The Health Squad Guide to Health and Fitness

Published 2005 by Onstream Publications Ltd
Currabaha, Cloghroe, County Cork, Ireland
Tel +353 21 4385798
Website: www.onstream.ie

Editing: Roz Crowley
Design: Nick Sanquest
Photography: Kieran Harnett
Food photography: Petra Carter
Photos: Pages 84,85: Nova Development Corporation

Photographed on location at Kelly's Resort Hotel & Spa, Rosslare, Co. Wexford, Ireland

Printed by Nicholson & Bass

ISBN: 1 89768 570 X

A CIP catalogue record for this book is available from the British Library

The publishers wish to thank ***safe*food**, the Food Safety Promotions Board, for their support and access to information and research resources.

***safe*food's** contribution to this book has solely been focused on offering nutritional advice. ***safe*food's** involvement does not constitute an endorsement of the opinions expressed, or other subjects covered in this publication. For further information on ***safe*food**, log on to www.safefoodonline.com

Health Squad is produced for RTÉ by Nemeton Television Productions

The advice and information in this book are based on the expertise of the authors. These writings are not intended as a substitute for professional advice. Anyone who has a medical condition or is concerned about their health should consult with their GP. The publisher, ***safe*food**, RTÉ, Nemeton and the authors specifically disclaim any liability, loss or risk, personal or otherwise, which is incurred, directly or indirectly, as a result of the use and application of the contents of this book.

The Health Squad Guide to Health and Fitness

Paula Mee
Pádraig Murphy
Karen Ward

ON STREAM

Imagine this: you are fit, full of energy and brimming with good health! That is where we all want to be, but never seem to get there without a little push.

This is what *Health Squad* is all about as Paula, Karen and Pádraig guide people towards healthier living. They do it so well that it seems to happen without having to make radical lifestyle changes.

Getting fit and healthy is easy, but many feel daunted by the prospect of making the vital changes. In this book, the Health Squad shows us how to change our lives for the better in easy steps. No radical changes, no backbreaking challenges, just simple effective adjustments to our lives such as eating the right foods, taking the right amount of exercise and looking after ourselves.

In these times of unhealthy, unhappy, overworked people, Paula, Karen and Pádraig have, through *Health Squad*, helped many people to change their lives. Not only have they done this, but in the process, they have been a pleasure to work with.

On television, *Health Squad* has been one of RTÉ's most successful home-produced lifestyle programmes over the past four years and its huge audience is very rewarding for us programme makers. This book builds on this experience and expands on the topics explored on the TV series.

Only here will you get the combined experience of all three Health Squad members coming together as mentors to guide you along your path.

Are you up for it? If you have picked up this book, chances are that you're already committed, you want to go further and you want the kind of personal success seen on the TV series.

If so, carry on reading and join the many people who, through *Health Squad* have achieved new healthier lives for themselves. I know this book will do the same for you.

Irial Mac Murchú
Managing Director
Nemeton Television Productions

Contents

Paula Mee

Pádraig Murphy

Karen Ward

Paula Mee has a BSc in Biochemistry, postgraduate qualifications in Dietetics, a Masters in Health Science from Leeds Metropolitan University and a Diploma in Allergy from Southampton University. She has completed the British Dietetic Association's Sports Dietitian course. Her company, Fruition, offers organisations and industry an extensive range of services in nutrition, product development and marketing communications. She operates a dietetic and weight management clinic at the Dublin Nutrition Clinic. She is currently on the board of Consumer Foods in Bord Bia, and is a member of the consultative council of the Food Safety Authority of Ireland.

Pádraig Murphy has worked in the health and fitness field for the past thirteen years. He became the first European to qualify as a Medical Exercise Specialist with the American Academy of Fitness Professionals. He has worked as a personal trainer to some of the leading figures in showbusiness and provided post-operative exercise care to national and international rugby teams. He has developed and presents a module on exercise in Trinity College Dublin on their Masters degree in Sports Medicine. He has held national titles in full contact kick-boxing and represented his country internationally. Pádraig works as a Sports Therapist in the Sea Spa at Kelly's Resort Hotel in Wexford.

Karen Ward is a Holistic Therapist. She has an honours degree in Biology from UCD and holds many holistic health qualifications including Holistic Psychotherapy, Stress Management Counselling, Reflexology and Aromatherapy Massage. She is also a Holistic Dietitian, a Yoga teacher, a Body Sculpting and a Pilates instructor. She runs her Clinic in Smithfield, Dublin with her sisters, Valerie and Pamela. She is a Reiki Master (USUI) and now practises Energy Therapy following on from her Shamanic studies. Her Yoga classes have run throughout Dublin for the last ten years and she now teaches Yoga on weekends and holidays.

health•squad

Understanding how the body works and deals with food is the job of the dietitian. While the availability of information increases, we have just as much misinformation which at times seems to be designed to confuse. When you read the quick-fix promises on the backs of countless diet books, it's hardly surprising that they capture the imagination of millions of people. Who doesn't want more energy, a strengthened immune system, a slimmer waistline, vanishing cellulite and a cleansed and healthy digestive system? And wouldn't it be great if we could achieve all that as well as a perky Kylie-like derrière in just six weeks, as we relentlessly indulge in our favourite foods? I do believe in fairies!

Paula

In the real world there are many of us who struggle with weight-related heart disease, diabetes and digestive disorders. In fact over half the population is overweight or obese. As a dietitian, I can't help but feel overwhelmed at times when I look at the incidence of obesity in Irish children and the future projections.

We make millions of food choices throughout our lives which have a major impact on our health and nutrition. Good food choices won't leave you and your family feeling unsatisfied, hungry or deprived, instead, they will make you feel in control and in charge of your life, as well as give you energy, a strengthened immune system and a slimmer waistline.

The good news is that food that is good for us tastes good too. The problem is we have been seduced into believing that we save time in using convenience foods. The real truth is that it's just a matter of stocking up on foods which don't take much preparation, but which deliver far more satisfaction in terms of appetite and keeping us going for long periods of time between meals. When we eat a lot of so-called convenience foods, we get more sugar, fat and salt but very little to sustain us. We feel hungrier sooner and end up eating far too much for our size.

The following chapters deliver some simple messages that can help prolong our lives, prevent heart disease and certain types of cancer. This is not about living an austere existence and not enjoying life. My recipe for life is about making the most of it, having fun, using what is readily available and not expensive. Eating well adds to our quality of life and optimises all that good health can offer. It's not complicated, and I hope the following pages will show just how simple it can be.

ENERGY: BOOSTERS AND ROBBERS

Some people seem to sail through a busy day and still have energy to spare at the end of it. In the search for stamina we need to make sure to exercise, have time to unwind and recharge the batteries and, inevitably, do an audit of the kitchen presses.

Energy is measured in either joules or calories. We tend to use the term calories in this country and as we use large amounts of energy, we use larger units called kilocalories (or kcal for short) to express how much energy we need or how much energy is found in 100g of a particular food.
All foods and most drinks contain calories which we can use as an energy source. The nutrients that provide us with energy (calories) are carbohydrates, fats and protein.

For optimum health, it is recommended that approximately half our energy should come from carbohydrates (these should be mainly wholegrain and low on the Glycaemic Index (*GI* see p.27) and not from protein as many celebrity diets suggest. Starchy foods such as the wholemeal versions of pasta, breakfast cereal, rice and bread, and potatoes provide fibre, vitamins and minerals, as well as energy. Our bodies run most efficiently when carbohydrate is burned as a fuel. It is more difficult to utilise fat and protein as energy sources.

Endless cups of coffee throughout the day temporarily improve alertness but only by stimulating an increase in blood glucose and adrenalin. It also appears that we can get so used to our regular caffeine fix that it becomes less effective with time. Moderate caffeine intake (2–3 cups of coffee per day) doesn't appear to cause problems in most healthy people, but if you drink more than this and you want to cut down, it's best to do so gradually in order to avoid withdrawal symptoms such as irritability, nausea, headaches and mood swings. Space out your caffeinated drinks over longer and longer periods, then make them weaker and finally replace them with water, herbal teas, fruit juices or smoothies.

Too much alcohol, although it contains calories, also saps energy. It robs the body of vital vitamins, especially B vitamins, which play an important part in releasing energy from food. In excess, it causes high blood pressure and its diuretic action can dehydrate the body, causing tiredness and headache. On the other hand, moderate drinking is associated with decreased risk of heart disease and lower overall mortality. It's back to a little of what you fancy…

Energy Boosters

Have a carbohydrate-rich breakfast to kick-start your day

Porridge or muesli with low fat milk, fruit or fruit juice.

Small protein-rich lunch

Sushi; tinned tuna or warm chicken salad; feta cheese on rye crackers with watercress or baby spinach leaves and vinaigrette; hummus and tomato on a toasted English muffin.

Low GI carbohydrates for your evening meal

Pasta salad or hot pasta main course; low fat yoghurt; pear, apples, grapes.

Energy boosting snacks

Oatcakes or flapjacks instead of ordinary biscuits or cakes; milk, 100% fruit juice and smoothies; raw veggies and low fat dip.

A good night's sleep

Fresh air during lunch or break

Eight large glasses of water every day

Exercise

Walk briskly; meditate; listen to music or get into the garden to unwind.

Energy Robbers

Excessive alcohol

A safe limit is 14 units (women) and 21 units (men) over the week; have one or two alcohol-free days.

Smoking

Robs you of precious energy; makes extra work for the antioxidants which detoxify the body; speeds up the rate at which you use up B vitamins and Vitamin C (smokers need twice as much Vitamin C as non-smokers).

Stress

Causes fatigue, digestive problems, lowered immunity and loss of appetite.

Iron deficiency anaemia

A lack of iron to transport oxygen and release energy from the cells can lead to chronic fatigue; tannin in tea and coffee can interfere with the absorption of iron, so avoid these drinks at mealtimes.

Seasonal Affective Disorder (SAD)

Thyroid Disorders

Depression

Fatigue

Can be a symptom of a gluten intolerance when iron is not absorbed from the damaged gut.

BREAKFAST FOODS

It's true that people who eat breakfast regularly stay slimmer, are more mentally alert and may even live longer than those who don't eat breakfast.

Skipping breakfast, for many people, might seem like the easiest way to trim their waistlines. However running out the door without breakfast can actually make losing weight more difficult!

Scientists continue to explore this peculiarity. It may be because the brain needs glucose to function and if we don't eat after a night's fast, the liver starts to produce glucose for the brain from its limited stores. Hormones are then produced to alert the body of its hunger and its need for carbohydrate which can be broken down into glucose. If we skip breakfast, by the time we get around to eating, the liver has taken care of our glucose needs and the carbohydrate we eat is converted into triglycerides, the precursor to fat cells. To help prevent these unwanted fat cells from forming the best thing we can do is eat breakfast. In the long run, the calories we eat during the day are better distributed, instead of being eating all at once. Develop good family habits by sitting down to breakfast each day.

GOOD BREAKFAST CHOICES

Having breakfast is vital, but so too is what you eat. The following are nine core breakfast foods for your shopping list:

1. Wholegrain Cereals or Breads

Research suggests that the risk of heart disease and type 2 diabetes can be up to 30% lower in people who regularly eat wholegrains as part of a low fat diet and healthy lifestyle.

The risk of cancer of the digestive tract may also be lower with higher intakes of wholegrains. These grains provide a food source for the 'friendly' gut bacteria which helps them to thrive and produce short-chain fatty acids which protect the gut wall.

Wholegrain cereal tends to have a lower Glycaemic Index (GI) than more refined processed cereals. This means they provide a steady slow release of sugar into the blood which, along with the fibre, helps to keep you feeling fuller for longer. (See *The GI guide to shaping up*, p. 27)

Wholegrains contain up to 75% more nutrients than refined cereals. They contain two different types of fibre: *soluble* (which helps to lower cholesterol levels and promote healthy gut bacteria) as well as the *insoluble* type (which helps with the regular movement of food through the intestine, avoiding constipation and other bowel disorders).

They provide us with B vitamins and folic acid.

They contain small amounts of minerals such as magnesium, zinc, phosphorous and iron.

They are also a source of antioxidants including vitamin E and selenium and phytonutrients such as phytoestrogens (lignans).

What does wholegrain mean?

There are many different cereal crops grown around the world such as wheat, rye, barley, oats, rice, triticale and buckwheat. Wholegrains are the seeds of these cereals. They contain a fibre-rich outer layer called the bran, a nutrient-packed inner part called the germ, and a starchy centre called the endosperm. Much of the goodness is found in the bran and germ but these are often removed to give a whiter more refined cereal.

2. Oats

Oats are super wholegrains that are naturally low in saturated fat and salt. They have a low glycaemic index which means a bowl of porridge can keep us feeling fuller for longer after breakfast, compared to other more processed cereals.

Oats are high in soluble fibre. This type of fibre works like a sponge, soaking up cholesterol-based bile acids and transporting them out of the body. The liver then takes more cholesterol out of the blood stream to replace the lost bile acids and the blood cholesterol levels drop, keeping the arteries clear and the heart healthy.

3. Probiotic Yoghurt

Yoghurt is an excellent source of bone minerals. Low fat live probiotic yoghurts contain very little saturated fat and lots of 'friendly bacteria' which produce enzymes that can be absorbed through the gut wall and enhance the immune system. (See *Immune Enhancers* p. 39).

4. Milk

Milk is another excellent bone food. Low fat varieties with protective omega 3 fats are now available on the supermarket shelf. The calcium in milk is easily absorbed, unlike the calcium found in plant foods. Choose a low fat milk if slimming. (See *Bone Foods* p. 60).

5. Fresh fruit or citrus fruits or frozen berries

Fruit is packed with phytochemicals, antioxidant vitamin C plus carotenoids, folate and fibre. Fruit is naturally low in fat, has very few calories and is a great energy-boosting start to the day. (See *What's a Phytochemical* p.45) Citrus fruits such as grapefruits and oranges are excellent sources of vitamin C. It's estimated they also contain more than 150 different phytochemicals, many of which have disease-fighting properties. These citrus fruits are particularly protective against cancer of the mouth, throat and stomach. They can also help to lower our risk of heart disease and stroke when eaten daily.

Berry fruits are rich sources of phytoestrogens and many antioxidants, including Vitamin C. Blueberries are top of the list of fruits and vegetables in their antioxidant activity. Scientists are researching their potential in slowing the ageing process, protecting our arteries by reducing harmful cholesterol levels and protecting against age-related conditions such as Alzheimer's disease.

6. Dried fruits

There is now a great assortment of dried fruit available in supermarkets and health shops, from the familiar plump raisin to the more exotic cranberry, papaya and mango. They provide great variety, new tastes and a burst of instant sweetness to the porridge bowl. They also contain significant amounts of iron, potassium and selenium, as well as fibre and vitamin A. More than can be said of table sugar!

7. Mixed seeds

Seeds are nutritional nuggets. They are rich in protective unsaturated fats, fibre, some B vitamins, Vitamin E and phytochemicals. Pumpkin and sunflower seeds are good sources of zinc and copper. Linseed (or flax seed) is a rich source of omega 3 fats and lignans (a type of phytoestrogen) which may help to relieve menopausal symptoms and reduce the risk of cancer.

8. Mixed nuts

Many nuts contain 50% fat (except chestnuts which are only 3% fat). However, most of the fat in nuts is protective, unsaturated fat. As they are so nutrient dense, yet high in calories, you only need small amounts to benefit from their antioxidants such as Vitamin E and selenium, their iron and their essential fatty acids.

9. Eggs

Eggs are full of protein, B vitamins, iron, zinc and Vitamins A, D and E. They also contain choline and biotin for healthy skin and hair. If blood cholesterol is normal, you can enjoy an egg a day if you wish. If you have high cholesterol, restrict intake to 3 a week. Obviously the healthiest way to enjoy them is without adding fat, so boil, poach or scramble in a non-stick pan.

An average bowl of chocolate-covered breakfast cereal contains as much sugar as a chocolate bar and has negligible amounts of fibre.
These are desserts not breakfast cereals!

You can get four times more salt in a bowl of certain cereals than you'd find in a 25g bag of roasted peanuts. There are new cereals now with little or no salt.
Read the labels.

Tips

Mix four or five of your favourite seeds together and store them in an airtight container. Keep them beside your oats and breakfast cereals. Continually top up the stores and scatter over cereals, salads or in breads.

You can do the same thing with your favourite nuts and dried fruits. If you have one large container, mix the nuts, dried fruit, seeds, wheatgerm and porridge oats together, and have homemade muesli ready for use.

If you don't like the thought of washing up porridge pots, buy the 2-minute microwaveable porridge oats and all you have to do is pop the bowl in the dishwasher.

Frozen berries are really delicious in breakfast smoothies and you don't have to remember to defrost them. Just pop them in and there's no need for ice cubes.

Homemade Muesli

Add 1 dessertspoon of mixed nuts (brazil nuts, flaked almonds, hazelnuts), 1 dessertspoon of mixed seeds (sesame, sunflower, linseed, pumpkin, etc.), 1 dessertspoon of dried fruit (raisins, apricots, cranberries), and 1 dessertspoon of wheatgerm to some porridge oats and serve with milk or low fat yoghurt.

Porridge with Apple Juice

Pour apple juice over porridge oats in a large bowl, cover and chill over night. Microwave the next morning and serve with yoghurt.

Porridge and Cranberries

Put oats in a microwaveable bowl, add in milk or water, stir in a tablespoon of dried cranberries (or any dried fruit). They will plump up as the porridge is microwaved. Enjoy their added sweetness with a splash of milk.

Mango and Oats Smoothie

Put 1 pot of natural yoghurt into a blender with mango (or any fresh fruit), 2 tablespoons of oats and 4 ice-cubes and blend until smooth.

Melon Medley

Combine slices of ripe mango, chunks of melon, chopped dried apricots, hazelnuts and a sprig of fresh mint, drizzle with a little lime juice and sprinkle with cinnamon. This is a great way to start the day with Vitamin A.

Carrot and Ginger Juice

A glass of carrot and ginger juice is an excellent source of carotenoids for those who eat breakfast on the run.

Bio-Yoghurt with Berries

Eating bio-yoghurts containing acidophilus or bifidus will help maintain a healthy gut flora and therefore ensure we make enough Vitamin K in the body. This is particularly useful if you are taking antibiotics because some of them inhibit the absorption of Vitamin K.

Orange juice

If you drink a lot of tea, it could be interfering with your iron uptake. Substitute your breakfast cup with a glass of orange juice, which is high in Vitamin C, to boost the immune system.

BEFORE THE BELL RINGS...

A ten minute breakfast every day will improve children's memory, focus and concentration. Children who eat breakfast tend to perform better in school. They simply don't concentrate well when they're hungry. Many studies have demonstrated that breakfast eaters are likely to achieve higher grades, pay closer attention, participate more in class discussions and manage more complex academic problems, than those who skip breakfast.

Children who are chronically tired, not because they've had a few late nights, may need to boost their iron intake. Fortified cereals and porridge provide iron in the diet. The iron in these foods is better absorbed when a glass of Vitamin C rich orange juice is added to the breakfast meal.

SCHOOL LUNCHES

Getting children involved in making their own school lunch helps them to understand the basics of putting together any meal. Teach them to pick something from each of these four groups in order to get a wide range of essential nutrients.

Carbohydrate foods: bread, rolls or baps (wholegrain if possible), wraps, pitta bread, bread sticks, crackers.

Protein group: Cold meats such as ham/turkey/chicken, tuna or hummus.

Vitamins and Minerals: Any fresh fruit, mini boxes of raisins, dried fruit like mango, apricots and dates, carrot sticks, salad veg.

Calcium: Yoghurt drinks, yoghurt pots, small cartons of milk, cheese cubes or strings.

Treat foods are occasional foods

Some schools have a policy on treats, others don't. Set limits on how many you feel is appropriate taking into account your child's energy needs.

Problems can arise when treats displace other, more nourishing, foods from a child's diet.

Treats: Mini chocolate bars, lower fat/salt crisps, mini muffins, cereal bars, brack, digestive biscuits.

School Lunch ideas

Cereal Group	Fruit & Veg	Milk Group	Meat Group	'Treats'
Brown bread	Bunch of seedless grapes	Yoghurt drink	Cold meat of choice	Mini muffin
Pitta pocket	Salad and 2 Satsumas	2 low fat fromage frais	Deli turkey	Fruit cake/brack
Soft roll or bagel	Smoothie	Cheddar cheese portion	Tuna and sweetcorn mix	Oatmeal cookie
Breadsticks	Banana	Fruit bio-yoghurts	Hummus dip	Popcorn
Wholegrain roll or bap	Carrot sticks	Small yoghurt drink	Hardboiled egg and mayo	Chocolate rice cake

Drinks

- Keep water readily accessible in the fridge. Refrigerating ordinary tap water (in fashionable water bottles) increases its appeal to children.
- Make sure your child has a personal, distinctive water bottle to take to school, the playing field or when travelling. This constant reminder will cue children to drink water when thirsty.
- As an alternative to fizzy soft drinks, make juice spritzers by mixing half of 100% juice with half sparkling water for parties or picnics.
- Cut into cubes any citrus fruit past its best that's still sitting in your bowl e.g. oranges, lemons and limes. Freeze them and pop them into still or sparkling water to give it an extra zing.

Parent's tips for feeding older children

Make up your own healthy snack list with your children. Stick it on the fridge or notice board.

Bring your children food shopping and get them to find and weigh fruits and vegetables and other foods you want them to take notice of.

Teach your children to cook.

Have a 'kids in charge' night where they are responsible for menu planning, cooking and the clean-up!

Set limits (with their agreement) on the amount of TV they watch.

Discuss food advertising with your children.

Tip

The more yellow the banana, the easier it is to digest. Greener bananas are more difficult to break down because the starch has not yet turned into sugar.

LUNCH

For many, finding time to eat a healthy lunch at work or at home may be even more challenging than finding ten minutes for breakfast. But since we eat about one-third of our daily calories at lunch, it's important to find ways to make that meal nutritious.

And what's so important about lunch? Again, the body needs energy, this time to get you through the afternoon. And even if you're not physically active, the brain needs to be fed. Like all balanced meals it's important to try and eat a variety of foods which will give you: carbohydrate for brain fuel, protein for alertness, a little fat to provide us with fat-soluble vitamins and essential fatty acids. On top of this we need a smattering of micronutrients (vitamins, minerals and phytochemicals) to keep us optimally nourished. What you eat for lunch can either boost energy levels or leave you feeling sleepy and easily distracted. Lunch, comprising carbohydrates with a low GI (brown bread, brown pasta, chick peas, beans) and foods high in protein (meat, eggs, fish, cheese), appears to produce greater alertness and more focused attention than high fat lunches. Protein-rich foods also trigger the sensation of fullness faster than fatty foods. This means that eating some protein at lunch can help to keep hunger at bay until dinner.

So, even if you can only manage a 15 minute break, take it! You'll be much more productive at what you're doing in the afternoon and your body will thank you for it in the long run.

10 Foods for Lunch

1. Avocado pear

Many slimmers shy away from avocados, but, calorie for calorie, they offer a super array of nutrients. The avocado is rich in potassium for a healthy blood pressure and the antioxidant Vitamin E which keeps nerves and skin healthy. See *Slowing the Signs of Ageing* P. 37) It contains protective monounsaturated fats similar to those found in olive oil which help to protect against heart disease and certain cancers. It also contains Vitamin B6 which may help with mood swings before menstruation.

TIP

If your avocado is not quite ready to eat, help it ripen more quickly by putting it in a paper bag with an apple.

2. Sardines and salmon

Fresh oily fish with dark flesh such as mackerel, tuna, sardines and salmon are the most concentrated sources of protective omega 3 fats which help to prevent our blood from clotting and keep our heartbeat regular. Canned sardines and salmon are good sources of protein and calcium as long as you eat the bones! The canning process can result in loss of omega 3 oils in tuna.

3. Cheese

Cheese is a good source of protein and an excellent provider of easy-to-absorb calcium. It is also an important source of zinc and Vitamin B12 for vegetarians. On the down side, many types of cheese are high in fat, so moderation is the key. Luckily hard cheeses such as Parmesan have strong flavours and shaving the cheese with a potato peeler makes it go a bit further. Cheddar is approx 35% fat, camembert/brie 26% fat, ricotta 11% fat and cottage cheese 4% fat or less.

4. Hummus

Made from chickpeas, hummus is a great source of protein and soluble fibre. This helps to lower harmful cholesterol and protect against heart disease. Chickpeas also contain potassium which can help control blood pressure, as well as folic acid which helps to lower homocysteine levels. High homocysteine levels increase the risk of heart disease and stroke.

5. Tomatoes

Tomatoes just blush with goodness! They are good sources of Vitamin C and beta-carotene and are by far the richest source of the antioxidant lycopene. A low lycopene level is associated with prostate cancer. Tomatoes contain other phytochemicals which, together with their lycopene levels, make them an important weapon in the fight against cancer. This is one case where processing can actually enhance the availability and absorption of nutrients. So enjoy a fresh tomato as well as a little salad tomato dressing, tomato purée, tomato soup or even tomato sauce!

6. Green Leafy Salads

These superfoods are packed with Vitamin C, beta-carotene, folic acid and fibre. Leafy vegetables such as spinach are also rich in lutein and zeaxanthin which are two antioxidants called carotenoids. High intakes of these protective phytochemicals may reduce the risk of age-related macular degeneration, the leading cause of blindness in people aged over fifty. Unfortunately the oxalic acid in spinach binds to its iron and calcium and neither of these two minerals are well absorbed from salad leaves.

7. Bean salads

Beans and pulses are naturally low in fat and contain no cholesterol. They are useful providers of many minerals and trace elements as well as protein. Beans contain soluble fibre and have a low GI so they can help you maintain a stable blood glucose level and keep you feeling fuller for longer after lunch. There's a growing variety of dried or canned and ready-to eat bean salads available in supermarkets and health stores.

8. Sprouts

Sprouts are concentrated sources of plant enzymes, vitamins, minerals and phytochemicals such as gluconasturtin which may help smokers fight cancers. They are actively growing seedlings and therefore retain more of their nutrients than other vegetables which start to lose their vitamin content as soon as they are picked. You can buy them as ready-to-eat mixes of broccoli, alfalfa, clover and radish or you can sprout them yourself at home. You can add them to salads, sandwiches and stir-fries.

9. Couscous

Couscous is a convenient, low fat source of energy. It contains a little iron and other minerals. Quick and easy to prepare (just add boiling water or stock), chopped vegetables and lots of herbs can be added to create a low fat, high fibre meal, rich in antioxidants, in minutes.

10. Water/Juices

We need water to get rid of waste from the body, to control our core temperature and to replace losses from breathing and sweating. In our moderate climate, we need about 8–11 glasses a day depending on the weather and how much exercise we take. If you don't have time to think about consistently re-hydrating during the day, try to get into the habit of drinking water before or after lunch.

Quick and easy lunch ideas

Spinach salad and chilli dressing

Add a little crushed garlic, sundried tomato paste, olive oil and chilli powder into half a tub of Greek yoghurt. Whisk well to combine. Drizzle the dressing over some washed baby leaf spinach and add a snip of parsley. Toss together and serve.

Simple hummus

Drain one can of chickpeas. Add a crushed clove of garlic and the zest and juice of half a lemon to the chickpeas and whiz in a blender. Drizzle in 2 tablespoons of olive oil and continue whizzing. Spoon mixture into a bowl and add some chopped olives and a pinch of paprika. If the hummus is too thick for your taste, add a tiny bit of cold water and whiz again in blender.

Couscous and chickpea salad

Put 200g of couscous in a bowl and pour over 200ml of hot vegetable stock. Cover and leave for 5 minutes. Halve a lemon and squeeze. Pour into an empty jar with 2 tablespoons of olive oil and 1 teaspoon of soya sauce. Seal and shake well. Drain chickpeas, finely chop a red onion and quarter a few cherry tomatoes. Add lots of fresh mint, basil, parsley and the dressing to the couscous. Stir well and season with black pepper. Serve straight away.

Sardines on toast

Preheat the grill. Toast 2 slices of nutty seedy wholegrain bread on both sides. Slice a tomato. Drain the tinned sardines leaving a little olive oil. Lay the tomato slices and sardines on the toast and squeeze over a little lemon juice. Grill for 2 minutes.

Salmon and eggs

Make a tasty omelette with 2 eggs, a splash of milk, some flaked fresh or canned salmon, chopped chives. Grate a tiny bit of your favourite cheese on top.

DINNER

An increasing number of lifestyle trends are tipping the weighing scales in the wrong direction. Many of us sit for most of the day. Others skip breakfast, have a light lunch and end up eating more than necessary later on in the evening. Unintentionally we eat lots of calories while absorbed in a television programme as we are hardly aware we are eating.

Maintaining a healthy weight is important to avoid carrying the extra kilograms which put the lungs, heart and joints under pressure. Losing a few kilograms can lessen the many health problems that go hand in hand with being overweight. And of course you'll have more energy to do the things you want to do.

The problem is that going on and off a diet again and again gets us nowhere in the long term. A far better idea is to reduce normal portion sizes and substitute healthier foods for the less healthy. There's no need to make drastic unsustainable changes. When we eat nutritionally-better food, we are less hungry.

Dinner can be the most heart-friendly meal of the day.
(See *Heart Health* p.52)

TV and Activity

Children need 60 minutes of physical activity every day. Set limits on the amount of TV they watch. TV viewing poses a double hazard. Firstly it displaces activity and secondly it exposes children to countless ads for less nutritious foods. The Kaiser Foundation in the US reviewed 40 studies on obesity and TV viewing. It found that the more TV children watched, the more likely they were to be overweight or obese. The link had even more to do with the ads these children watched, more so than the fact that they were inactive. Other children who were just as sedentary (reading or playing board games) were not as overweight or obese as those who watched TV. Perhaps this is an opportunity for food companies advertising healthier foods and snacks?

In 2005 a Cork and Kerry study reported that:

- 1/3 of children had a TV in their room
- 1/3 of families ate meals in front of the TV
- Most children got less than 40 minutes of actual PE in a week
- 40% of schools banned running in the school yard.

10 Core foods for the dinner shopping list

1. Tuna or any oily fish

You can enjoy lots of variety here – tuna, trout, mackerel, salmon or sardines. The omega 3 fats protect against heart disease by reducing the risk of clots, lowering harmful LDL cholesterol and keeping the heart beat regular. Research has found that eating oily fish twice a week can reduce the risk of stroke by 18%. Oily fish can also reduce the inflammation associated with osteoarthritis. A recent study found that older people who ate oily fish once a week had a 60% lower risk of Alzheimer's than those who rarely or never ate it.

2. Cruciferous Vegetables

Broccoli, cabbage, green beans, kale, pakchoi, spinach and Brussels sprouts are all part of this family of vegetables that contain a number of phytochemicals including indoles, isothyocynates and sulphuraphane which seem to have anti-cancer properties. (See *Cancer Defence Boosters* p.43) Like all vegetables, they are naturally low in fat, high in fibre and many are good sources of folate, riboflavin and potassium.

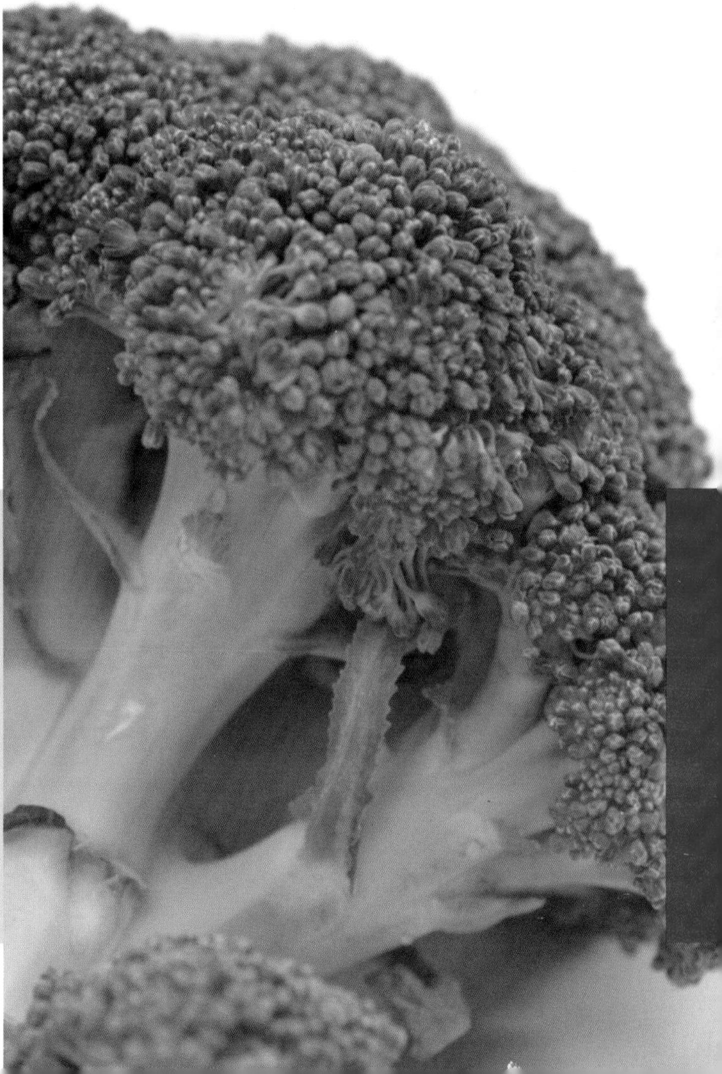

TIP

Choose very green florets of broccoli, not yellowy green ones. Beta-carotene makes the broccoli green, so go for the darkest with the maximum amounts of antioxidant.

3. Almonds

Almonds contain the healthy monounsaturated type of fat, similar to that found in olive oil. They also contain potassium which helps control blood pressure and the powerful antioxidant Vitamin E which has anti-ageing properties. Studies have found that people who regularly eat nuts have a lower risk of heart disease, so replace some of the harmful saturated fats you eat with a handful of unsalted nuts now and then.

4. Beef

Lean beef is an excellent source of protein, iron and zinc, the latter two minerals being particularly well absorbed. In fact, the iron in meat is seven times more easily absorbed than it is from vegetables. Beef and other red meats are a good source of chromium, which is needed for insulin to function properly in order to control blood glucose levels.

5. Olive oil

Olive oil contains monounsaturated fats which can lower harmful LDL cholesterol without lowering the beneficial HDL cholesterol. Along with lots of fruits, vegetables, fish, nuts and wholegrain, this Mediterranean style of dining can cut the risk of premature death by 25%.

6. Soya

Soya beans are a good source of protein, fibre and the minerals potassium, phosphorous, iron and calcium. Products containing them, such as tofu, are useful in a wide range of recipes. Miso and soya sauce have strong flavours and a little adds a touch of the orient to a stir-fry. Phytoestrogens found in soya mimic human oestrogen and reduce cholesterol levels. Their long term consumption may reduce breast cancer risk and may be beneficial for bone health.

7. Garlic

Garlic is renowned for its antiviral, anti-fungal and antibiotic properties. When you crush or chop garlic, a substance called allicin is released. This helps to prevent blood clots and reduces harmful cholesterol. Scientists recommend that you leave about fifteen minutes between crushing and cooking to maximise the health benefits of allicin.

8. Pasta and Rice

Pasta, made from durum wheat, has a low GI and is an excellent low fat source of slowly released energy. However, like all grains, the more refined it is, the fewer nutrients there are, so wholewheat varieties are best. Many of the nutrients like Vitamin B are also removed from white rice, so choose a brown or wild rice with a low GI instead.

9. Herbs

Many potent medicines are derived from herbs and other plants. Although many herbs contain Vitamin C and phytochemicals such as carotenoids, they have little nutritional value because of the small amounts consumed. However herbs and spices are a healthy and tasty alternative to seasoning food with salt. (See *Salt belongs in the Sea* p.59) Their therapeutic properties come from the essential oils they contain and many, like mint and basil, seem to aid digestion as well as enhancing a salad.

10. Red Wine

Although heavy drinkers have a much higher risk of death, moderate drinkers have the lowest death rate, lower even than teetotallers. Red wine, in particular, protects against heart disease. It reduces blood clotting and raises the protective type of cholesterol HDL. But the key is moderation. The recommendation is for women to drink no more than 14 units (14 small glasses) and men 21 units (or 21 small glasses) in a week.

_safe_food tips

Keep vegetables as nutritious as possible by boiling vegetables in as little water as possible. Try steaming, microwaving (with a couple of tablespoons of water) or stir frying.

Avoid the fat attack: don't use the frying pan or deep fat fryer often and use olive oil for frying and vegetable fats for occasional deep-frying. Instead grill, use a griddle pan, steam or bake. The trick is not to add too much fat to your food when cooking.

Dinner Ideas

Cook pasta and toss with a pesto made with fresh rocket, almonds, grated Parmesan cheese and oil.

Lightly steam broccoli, drizzle with lime juice and sesame oil and finish with oyster sauce and slices of fried garlic.

Char-grill sirloin steak until medium rare, slice and serve on a bed of baby spinach topped with sliced char-grilled red pepper and parsley pesto.

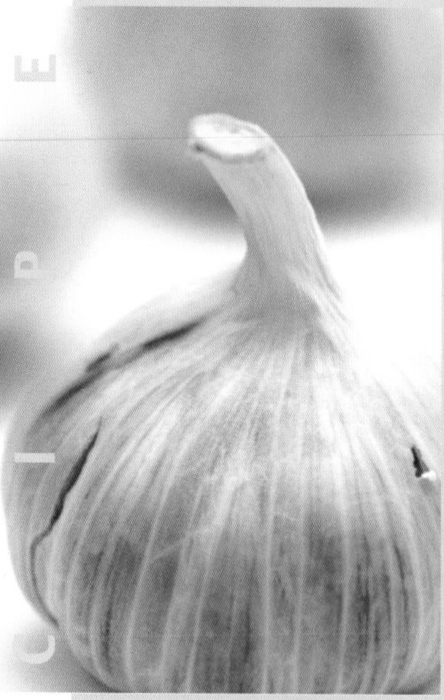

Garlic and Thyme Fish Steaks

Crush 2 garlic cloves and put in a large shallow container with 2 tablespoons roughly chopped thyme, 4 tablespoons olive oil and the juice of 1 lemon. Mix well. Add 4 fish steaks, such as tuna or swordfish. Season with salt and freshly ground black pepper. Cover and chill for 20 minutes. Cook the fish (reserving the marinade) in a preheated griddle pan for 4–5 mins each side. Cut another lemon into thin slices. Turn over the fish, brush with a little marinade and top each steak with a slice of lemon. Continue to cook for 3–4 minutes or until cooked through.

Smoked mackerel with potato and horseradish salad

Cook 6 potatoes in a pan of boiling water for 15–20 minutes or until tender. Drain and set aside. Mix together 1 tablespoon horseradish sauce, 1 tablespoon crème fraiche, 1 teaspoon lemon juice and 1 dessertspoon olive oil, then season. Roughly chop apples and warm potatoes, put in a large bowl and toss in the dressing. Skin and flake 2 fillets of mackerel and add to a bowl of watercress. Toss together and serve with the salad.

Sesame trout

Preheat the grill. Put 1 tablespoon sesame oil in a bowl. Add 1 tablespoon soya sauce and the juice of 1 lime and whisk together. Put 4 trout fillets on a baking sheet, pour over the sesame mixture and grill for 8 minutes. Sprinkle with 2 tbsp sesame seeds and grill again for 2 minutes until the seeds are golden. Serve with a wedge of lemon or lime and a green salad.

Fresh Tuna with Pasta and Green Beans

- 2 fresh tuna steaks
- 100g green beans (trimmed and halved)
- Half a red pepper, sliced thinly
- Two inches of courgette, sliced thinly
- 1 small red onion, sliced thinly
- 100g wholemeal pasta

Dressing: put the following ingredients into a bowl and mix well.

- 4 tablespoons olive oil
- 1 garlic clove, crushed
- 2 tablespoons lemon juice
- 2 tablespoons fresh chopped parsley

Cook the pasta and drain.

Steam, microwave or stir-fry the vegetables until cooked but still firm. Brush the tuna steaks with olive oil and sear in the pan, turning at least once, for 8 minutes. Break into chunks.

Put the tuna chunks, vegetables and pasta into a serving bowl. Pour over the dressing. Toss and serve immediately.

DEVELOPING GOOD FOOD HABITS

We know from the *National Children's Food Survey 2005* that what happens at home has the greatest influence on our children's nutritional intake. In other words, what's in the fridge, freezer and presses will dictate what the kids will eat.

Rather than starting a revolution, small, positive steps can all make a difference.

As parents, we can start with ourselves. We can formulate good eating and activity habits, provide quick but nourishing family meals and set limits on (not ban) foods with little nutritional value.

We can try to eat meals together. This is where we can talk and educate each other about different foods and how they can help us to grow and provide enough energy for play and to concentrate on getting the homework done quickly so they can enjoy other activities afterwards.

Slow eaters may need gentle encouragement, but don't get into the habit of spoon-feeding children who are well able to feed themselves.

Try to avoid telling children to 'take one more bite' or 'clean your plate' when they are full.

Young children may need to be offered a new food 8 to 10 times before they will accept it, yet the majority of parents with fussy eaters give up offering a new food if the child has not accepted it after 2 or 3 attempts. So the message is: PERSEVERE but don't pressurise.

Devise a healthy snack list with your children. Stick it on the refrigerator.

Teach your children to cook.

Assign children a 'Kids Rule' night where they are in charge of menu planning, cooking and clean-up.

Involve your children at the supermarket by giving them a list of foods to find. Add a few unusual foods to the list each time (for example, avocado, kale or hummus).

Encourage children to play outside whenever feasible. If you can play with them, all the better.

On the weekend, live life instead of watching it on TV. Find a new place to hike, bike or walk. Find an indoor swimming pool that you can use all year long.

Discuss food advertising with your children.

Teach your children how to read and understand the information on food labels.

Study a different culture and learn more about their lifestyle and eating habits. Or study Irish food habits over the years. Interview an older relative or visit the library or bookstore for authentic ethnic recipes and then prepare some new dishes together.

Enjoy eating a variety of foods!

Did you know?

A can of fizzy soft drink contains approx 11 cubes of sugar.

JUICE

A glass of fresh juice is a great way of getting one of your servings of fruit and vegetables every day.

Obviously fresh is best. You can invest in a juicer and make up your own. Latest versions of juicers have improved, leaving less pulp and fibre in the machine and more in the glass, where it belongs.

Failing that, buy the next best thing – there is a wide variety of unusual premium juices available in the local supermarket or health store: blueberry juices, aronia berry juices, cranberry juices.

Parents' tips for feeding young children

Where possible eat meals together. This is where we can try, taste and talk about new foods.

Young children may need to be offered a new food 8 to 10 times before they accept it, yet many of us parents give up if the child has not accepted it after 2 or 3 attempts. Persevere but don't pressurise.

Actions speak louder than words. Show your child how much you enjoy nutritious foods yourself.

Slow eaters may need gentle encouragement but don't get into the habit of spoon feeding children who can feed themselves.

FIZZY DRINKS

6 reasons to limit fizzy soft drinks for children.

To protect the bones

Studies show that children and teenagers who regularly consume large amounts of phosphorous-rich cola drinks are at greater risk of bone fractures than non-cola drinkers. Never allow fizzy soft drinks to replace milk!

To protect the teeth

The acidity of some fizzy soft drinks is about the same as vinegar. The sugar content masks the acidity which can cause tooth erosion.

To reduce stimulants

Fizzy soft drinks are the single greatest source of caffeine in children's diets. An average can of cola contains about 45 milligrams but the amounts in more potent colas can exceed 100 milligrams, a level closer to coffee.

To avoid weight gain

Consuming sugary (high fructose corn syrup) sweetened drinks is associated with a higher risk of obesity. Sugar sweetened soft drinks provide empty calories and have a high GI. A high GI diet may promote changes in blood sugar, hormones and appetite that can cause weight gain. A single can of fizzy soft drink contains approximately 11 cubes of sugar.

To avoid unnecessary additives such as artificial colours

Soft drinks contain preservatives and artificial colours such as Tartrazine and Sunset Yellow which a small but significant group of children may be sensitive to.

To reduce the risk of diabetes

Studies have found that people who drank at least one sugary drink each day had an 83 percent higher risk of diabetes than those who drank only one per month.

As an alternative to fizzy drinks *safe*food recommends

1. **Plain water**
2. **A glass of milk. (Flavoured milk or milk shakes count as treats: they contain added sugar.)**
3. **A glass of unsweetened fruit juice each day**

SHAPING UP WITH THE GLYCAEMIC INDEX

What's all the fuss about?

Dietitians have been using the Glycaemic Index for years to help diabetic patients to control their blood glucose levels. Elite athletes employ it to regulate their energy levels and stamina, and now it's become the most fashionable remedy for an expanding waistline.

But the GI is not about amazing celebrity shrinkage, deprivation or stunning inch loss in minutes, it's about understanding how certain foods can release their sugars slowly into the bloodstream, and supply a steady source of energy with no unruly peaks and troughs. Not all carbohydrates are the same. In the same way that not all fats are bad, not all carbohydrates are necessarily good for us either. Research continues to confirm that carbohydrates with a low GI are better for our hearts and our waistlines. They make us feel fuller for longer after we've eaten which helps us to eat fewer calories during the day.

With the sheer abundance of food choices we are faced with, the problem for many people is how to navigate the huge sea of calories around them. As dieting has become more contagious than measles, the GI Eating Guide will help you enjoy foods that are healthy and nutritious from each of the four major groups, ensuring an ample intake of fibre, vitamins, minerals, essential fats and phytonutrients. And you can lose weight too, without starving.

The new way to eat....

To begin with, let's not forget the basic rule of CICO.
Calories In must equal Calories Out for you to stay the same weight as you are now. But the fewer calories you eat and the more you burn off, the more weight you lose.

There are heaps of calories in alcohol and highly processed foods, chips, fried foods, soft drinks, biscuits, cakes, confectionery etc. These are the primary targets for elimination.

- Most of us eat too much sugar.
- Sugary foods and drinks can cause tooth decay.
- Many sugary foods contain calories but very few other nutrients.
- Eating sugary processed snacks can cause havoc with blood glucose and insulin control which is bad for our waistlines and our health.

You can still fill a plate with the same amount of food, it's just that these foods must contain a lot more water and fibre. Fruits and salad vegetables fill you up, without the calorific load.

Fad Diets

Weighing up the Facts

As you scour the bookshelves, take some time to ask yourself a few questions before you jump on the next 'revolutionary' diet bandwagon. See how the program holds up under scrutiny.

Does it:

- Promise a quick fix/miracle results/effortless weight loss in just a few weeks?
- Make claims that sound too good to be true? It probably is!
- Quote simplistic conclusions from a single study?
- Make remarkable statements that are refuted by reputable scientific organisations?
- Try to sell you slimming foods or products as well as the diet? Many so-called experts are usually good sales people. Be wary when someone tries to diagnose your health or weight problem and then in the next breath offers to sell you the remedy.
- Support its claims? Advice should be backed up by credible sources, independent research etc. Remember, one study isn't enough. Testimonials from people who tried the diet are not enough either.

Check their Credentials

Who wrote it and are they qualified in the field of nutrition and dietetics? Qualified nutrition and dietetic experts have specific academic and training credentials. They know the science of nutrition. Their degrees in nutrition, dietetics or public health come from well-respected universities. They may use the title dietitian or nutritionist to describe what they do. In Southern Ireland, you should seek out a member of the Irish Nutrition and Dietetic Institute (www.indi.ie) and in Northern Ireland and the UK a member of the British Dietetic Association (www.bda.uk.com).

You can enjoy moderate amounts of fats but regularly choose foods that contain monounsaturated fats (olive or rapeseed oil) and omega 3 fats (oily fish and linseeds) over saturated animal fats (butter, cream, hard cheese) and partially hydrogenated fats (biscuits, crackers, spreads).

It helps to divide your plate into four sections: two quarters for fresh or salad vegetables, one for protein-rich foods such as peas, beans, lentils, oily fish, white fish, turkey, chicken or lean red meat and the last quarter for low GI carbohydrates.

Nutrients don't all give us the same feelings of fullness or satiety. Their satiating power works as illustrated on the right.

...where protein and low GI carbohydrates have a greater ability to fill us for longer than fats

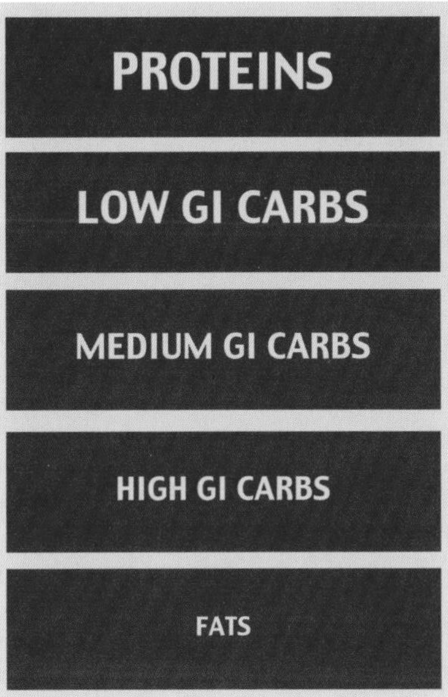

Did you know?

The brain needs at least a third of our daily calories to function well.

The neurons are more susceptible than the other parts of the body to both deficiencies and excesses.

Granny was right: Fish is good for our brains. If your child doesn't like oily fish (tuna, salmon, sardines and mackerel) try mixing a dessertspoon of ground linseeds into their breakfast cereal or use omega 3 enriched milk and eggs. A fish oil supplement is the next best thing.

LOW GI FOODS

Choose lots of low GI carbohydrates as your staples during the week. Eat plenty of fruits and vegetables from this group but think of pasta and rice as side orders (1/4 plate), rather than the main food on your plate.

Apples
Beans (green, runner)
Blueberries
Broccoli
Cabbage
Cannelloni beans
Cherries
Chickpeas
Citrus fruits
Grapes
Hummus
Kidney beans
Lentils
Milk (use skimmed or low fat)
Muesli (unsweetened)
Mushrooms
Noodles
Oat bran
Onions
Pasta (dried or fresh, wholemeal)
Peas
Pearl barley
Peaches
Pears
Peppers
Porridge oats
Quorn
Raspberries
Rhubarb
Strawberries
Tomatoes

MEDIUM GI FOODS

These are examples of foods which you can enjoy moderately. Some, however, such as chocolate, are high in saturated fat and calories, and therefore warrant further restrictions when slimming.

Basmati rice
Boiled potatoes
Chocolate
Couscous
Pineapple
100% wholegrain bread

Tip
Acidic fruits such as citrus fruits (lemons, oranges and grapefruits) have low GIs. Likewise lemon juice and vinegar (as in a salad dressing) can help to reduce the glycaemic load of the meal.

HIGH GI FOODS

These are examples of foods to aim to eat less often. They tend to be quickly absorbed into the bloodstream, triggering the pancreas to release lots of insulin and leave you feeling hungry again soon after you've eaten. There are some surprises here e.g. watermelon, carrots, parsnips. You can make an exception for these fruits and vegetables if you eat them as part of a meal with a high protein or good fat component because both protein and fat decrease the glycaemic load of the meal.

Bagels
Biscuits
Bread (brown and white sliced)
Breakfast cereals (refined)
Carrots
Cereal bars
Crispbreads
Croissants
Dates
Doughnuts
Jelly beans
Ketchup
Melon
Parsnips
Popcorn
Potatoes (mashed and baked)
Pretzels
Rice (white)
Rice cakes
Soft drinks (regular)
Watermelon

Think about it...

Frequently it's not food we're hungry for but:

- Relief from boredom
- Affection
- A way to relieve anger
- A way to deal with loneliness or stress

The basic point is if we address what we're really hungry for, we will be less tempted to turn to food to satisfy these hungers. Sometimes we assume we can only deal with certain issues, such as loneliness, depression, boredom, after we've first taken control of our diet and we're back to the weight we were twenty years ago. Yet it's a mistake to assume that dieting must come first. In fact we will be much more successful with the dieting if we are also learning to handle other problems in our lives.

So the next time you're hungry, satisfy it, but with what you are really hungry for!

Sugary muesli: how much sugar should we allow ourselves in it? When you're reading food labels, the following figures can give you a rough guideline:

- **A lot of sugar = 10g per 100g of food**
- **A little sugar = 2g per 100g of food**
- **A moderate amount of sugar = between 2g and 10g**

The amount of sugar in muesli is frequently high. Unfortunately the label won't tell how much of the sugars are naturally occurring in dried fruit and how much comes from added sugars. Therefore a good claim to watch out for on your muesli cereals is 'no added sugar' or 'unsweetened.' If you see this, the sugar content on the label will reflect natural sugars from dried or fresh fruit only.

Eleven Healthy Eating Reminders

1 Be prepared for the day you run out of fresh food. Always have the fridge, freezer and presses stocked with low GI foods such as frozen peas and green beans, frozen berries, frozen quorn, cans of kidney and cannelloni beans, oat bran, wholemeal pasta, basmati rice, porridge oats (for homemade muesli) and plenty of nuts and seeds.

2 Don't skip meals, especially breakfast.

3 If you get hungry in between meals, eat low GI fruit, some raw veg and hummus or a small handful of nuts to keep you going.

4 Get rid of processed white foods from the kitchen e.g. white bread and bagels, white rice and refined breakfast cereals.

5 Eating sugary processed snacks can cause havoc with blood glucose and insulin control which is bad for our waistlines and our health. Most of us eat too much sugar and sugary foods and drinks can cause tooth decay. Many sugary foods contain calories but very few other nutrients.

6 Choose wholemeal pasta and basmati, brown and unrefined rice instead. Try not to eat more than two slices of 100% wholegrain bread each day. Think variety!

7 Vegetables and salads should fill half the plate.

8 Don't over-cook, mash or purée food. This increases the GI of the food. Leave your body do most of the work, chewing well and slowly, digesting and absorbing the nutrients.

9 Eat more monounsaturated (olive/rapeseed) and omega 3 (oily fish) fats than saturated (butter, cream) or partially hydrogenated fats (spreads).

10 Don't fool yourself into thinking you can eat as much chocolate (medium GI) as you want without putting on weight. Likewise, you don't have to give up all high GI foods. Weight control is based on total calorie intake.

11 Don't throw away good fibre from plant foods by juicing. Stick to one small glass of juice each day and eat the rest of fruit and vegetables whole.

SAMPLE GI MENU

Breakfast
Bowl of unsweetened muesli.
Top it with low fat bio-yoghurt and berries or favourite seeds

Mid-morning
Apple, pear, orange or 12 grapes
500ml water (flavour with slices of lemon or lime)

Lunch break
Thick slice of goat's cheese or 2 heaped tablespoons of hummus.
Serve with salad of mixed leaves, thin slivers of red pepper, cucumber and half an avocado, sprinkled with pine nuts
500ml water

Mid-afternoon
Small handful (8–10) of your favourite nuts: cashew, walnut, pistachio
500ml of water

Dinner
Seared fresh tuna with pasta and green beans (See recipe p. 23).

The Glycaemic Load (GL) is a relatively new way to assess the impact of carbohydrate consumption that takes the glycaemic index (GI) into account, but gives a fuller picture than does the GI alone. A GI value tells you how rapidly a particular carbohydrate turns into glucose. It doesn't tell you how much of that carbohydrate is in a serving of a particular food. You need to know both things to understand a food's effect on blood sugar. That's why the GI should not be the only criterion when selecting what to eat. The total amount and type of carbohydrate, the amount and type of fat and protein, the fibre and salt content are also important.

The Highs and Lows of Diabetes

Once upon a time carbohydrates were either 'simple' or 'complex'. Simple carbohydrates such as honey, we thought, were quickly absorbed into the bloodstream and complex carbohydrates like bread were more slowly absorbed, because of their more complicated structure. The science was straightforward, or so it seemed.

Nowadays the Glycaemic Index (GI) of carbohydrates debunks this theory. It gives us a better measure of just how high and how quickly different carbohydrates raise blood glucose levels. As a result, we are beginning to grasp the effects of certain foods on hunger and appetite control. Foods can be classified as having a low, medium or high glycaemic index, and are ranked from zero to 100.

Based on these findings, we know our bodies can rapidly break down and convert a fast food meal containing high GI carbohydrates such as French fries, burger buns and soft drinks, into glucose. This glucose is absorbed into the bloodstream and spikes the glucose level there, resulting in a 'sugar high'. The problem arises after the spike, when glucose quickly disappears from the bloodstream leaving us feeling sluggish and hungry again. In effect, what happens is that the rapid spike signals the pancreas to release more insulin, a hormone which diverts the glucose from the blood into various body tissues. Here, it is either burned immediately or stored as fat. Insulin also stops our bodies from converting this fat back into glucose for the body to burn. Bad news for the waistline.

One of the most important implications of the GI factor is in the area of diabetes. Evidence suggests that replacing high GI foods with low GI ones can help patients control and regulate their blood glucose levels. In the past, people with diabetes were advised to avoid table sugar as it was thought to raise blood glucose levels rapidly. Current recommendations now allow a modest amount of table sugar, as the inclusion of a little sugar as part of a meal has little impact on either blood sugar or insulin concentrations.

Raised eyebrows or even whoops of joy can be expected when those with diabetes take a first glimpse at the list of low GI foods. Chocolate is better than wholemeal bread, table sugar is better than a baked potato. Fantastic! Unfortunately, this is not the correct interpretation. The GI table only classifies foods on the basis of their effect on blood glucose levels. Other factors such as how much fibre, vitamins and minerals and essential fatty acids the food contains are important.

Lowering the GI of the diet does not require the elimination of all high GI foods such as wholemeal bread, but it could signal that restraint is necessary if you tend to eat a lot of bread, and yet you're always hungry. So to feel satisfied, instead of having two or three slices of bread, you could eat one slice topped with baked beans. It also means when you have diabetes that you don't need to live in terror of a little bit of chocolate now and then. Just make sure you have it with a meal, that the diet is well balanced and that you're not watching your waistline!

It's essential that GI is kept in perspective and that it is remembered that all high carbohydrate foods can make an important contribution to a healthy well balanced diet. Whilst the World Health Organisation has endorsed the use of GI in the management of certain diseases, there isn't universal consensus on the merits of GI as yet. We still have work to do. We need to standardise the methods we use to measure GI for the correct interpretation and application of GI values in practice. Research is ongoing.

At least 39% of adults are overweight and a further 18% are classified as obese in Ireland. The 2005 *National Children's Survey* has also shown that approximately 1 in 5 children aged 5–12 is overweight or obese.

Additional calories from larger portion sizes is one of the most striking differences in the diets between normal weight or overweight/obese adults.

***safe*food recommends:**

- **Choose healthy snacks such as fruit.**
- **Increase the proportion of fruits and vegetables at each meal.**
- **Use a smaller plate. Plate sizes have been gradually increasing over the years and as a result we have been adding more food to get a 'plateful'.**
- **Eat more slowly and stop when you are full. This goes for children too – don't force them to finish all the food that is on their plate.**
- **Keep leftovers out of sight.**
- **If you are eating out don't go for 'go large' or 'supersize'.**

SLOWING THE SIGNS OF AGEING

It might be foolish of us to assume that by eating certain foods we can stop skin ageing, obliterate wrinkles and prevent skin cancer. But it's just as foolish to think that we can eat whatever we want, without it having any effect on our skin. Nutrition matters.

The skin, it's often said, is the outer reflection of our inner health. Much of the ageing of our skin is the result of long-term exposure to sun, tobacco smoke and ozone. Environmental pollutants generate highly destructive free radicals that damage collagen and consequently the skin's firmness and suppleness. The result is what dermatologists call photo-ageing, which includes dryness, loss of elasticity, and the appearance of fine lines and wrinkles. The free radicals generated by sun exposure can also damage the genetic structure of skin cells and contribute to the development of cancer. Antioxidant nutrients, including vitamins C, E and beta-carotene, slow down the rate of free-radical damage to the skin. Practically speaking, if you commit yourself to eating at least five or more antioxidant-rich foods each day – peppers, spinach, mangos, tomatoes, carrots – you can stockpile some of these health-enhancing nutrients in your tissues and help to lower the risk of premature skin ageing and cancer.

As uninspiring as it may sound, the diet optimal for overall health is comparable to the diet that is optimal for skin health. It slows down the physiological mechanisms of ageing in all tissues, including the skin. A deficiency of any nutrient, especially iron, can suffocate the skin and leave it pale and drawn.

Apart from frying your body in direct sunlight, another sure way to get wrinkles is to put on a lot of weight and then lose it again. All that extra fat stretches the skin, and then when we lose the extra pounds, the skin sags and wrinkles up.

Of course a well-moisturised skin is also somewhat less prone to developing wrinkles and looking aged. Drinking eight of more glasses of water throughout the day ensures proper hydration. Coffee and cola soft drinks are not good substitutes for water because they contain caffeine which promotes the loss of water in the urine. So stick to green tea which is full of antioxidants.

Feeding your Skin

Vitamin C helps build collagen, the ‘scaffolding’ between the tissues of our body. Poor intake of Vitamin C can cause bruising, loss of skin strength and elasticity, and poor healing of cuts and scrapes.
Sources: Just one daily glass of orange juice or bowl of strawberries supplies all the Vitamin C we need. Other excellent sources include blackcurrants, red peppers, curly kale, brussell sprouts, papaya, kiwi, satsumas, grapefruit and broccoli.

Vitamin A (precursor beta-carotene) maintains healthy epithelial tissues such as skin, thus helping to prevent premature wrinkling or bumpy, sandpaper-like skin.
Sources: liver, paté, carrots, margarine, butter, sweet potatoes, red/orange peppers, spinach, butternut squash, watercress, cheese.

Vitamin E, a powerful antioxidant which helps to prevent oxidation of polyunsaturated fatty acids in cell membranes and other tissues.
Sources: Wheat germ oil, sunflower oil, safflower oil, palm oil, hazelnuts, almonds, tomatoes, rapeseed oil, soya oil.

Essential Fatty Acids such as linoleic acid help restore damaged skin and maintain smooth, moist skin.
Sources: Anchovies, canola oil, cod liver oil, egg yolk, flaxseed oil, hazelnuts, mackerel, oysters, prawns, salmon, sardines.

Zinc helps to heal cuts and scrapes.
Sources: Beef, all seafood and the myco-protein *quorn*.

Flavonoid-rich foods are powerful anti-oxidants that fight free radicals. Sources: Proanthocyanins are found in grapes and pine nuts; polyphenols are found in green tea.

Selenium is part of the enzyme *glutathione peroxidase* which is involved in protecting body tissues against free radicals.
Sources: Brazil nuts, kidneys, mixed nuts and raisins, lobster, tuna, lemon sole, squid, mullet, scallops, sardines, hummus.

IMMUNE ENHANCERS

The immune system is highly evolved to protect us against invading organisms such as bacteria, viruses, parasites and fungi, and against our own cells that have become cancerous. To boost our natural defences we need to eat well. The immune system needs well over twenty different micro-nutrients to function properly. Fad diets and poorly-designed slimming diets can leave us vulnerable to infection, not only because of the calorie restriction which slows down our metabolism, but also because they can be low in essential nutrients such as antioxidants and natural protective phyto-nutrients found in plant foods. We need a consistent intake of these essential nutrients to keep our immune systems continually working to protect us from infections and diseases. A number of studies have shown that supplements of vitamins and minerals can improve immune function, particularly in the elderly.

Here are some of the more essential nutrients that are essential for a healthy immune system.

Nutrient: **Vitamin A** (found in animal products) and beta-carotene (found in plant foods) which is converted into Vitamin A in the body
Function: For reproduction and development. For healthy skin, hair and eyes. Helps the body resist infection and protects against cell damage.
Deficiency signs: Poor vision, scaly skin, poor growth and increased susceptibility to infection.
Food sources: Liver, fish, eggs, dairy products, mangoes, vegetables such as carrots, peppers, spinach and watercress
Synergists: Zinc, Vitamin D, some antibiotics
Inhibitors: Alcohol, a very low fat intake

Nutrient: **Vitamin B2** (Thiamin)
Function: Release energy from carbohydrates, fats and proteins. Vital for growth and vision and a healthy immune system
Deficiency signs: Poor wound healing, cracked lips and corners of mouth, flaking skin, rash between nose and lips
Food sources: Yeast extract, milk, cheese, yoghurt, eggs, meat, green leafy vegetables, fortified breakfast cereals
Synergists: Other B vitamins
Inhibitors: Destroyed by heat and light. Oral contraception pill, alcohol, some antidepressants

Nutrient: **Vitamin B6** (Pyridoxine)
Function: Release energy from protein. Essential for a healthy nervous and immune system
Deficiency signs: Depression, headaches, confusion, tingling in hands and feet, decreased antibody formation (immunity)
Food sources: Yeast extract, wholemeal bread, wheat germ, fortified breakfast cereal, liver, avocados, bananas, fish, meat
Synergists: Other B vitamins
Inhibitors: Exposure to heat and light, alcohol, oral contraception pill, smoking

Nutrient: **Vitamin C** (Ascorbic acid)
Function: Antioxidant which helps prevent cell damage caused by free radicals and pollutants such as cigarette smoke
Deficiency signs: Loss of appetite, muscle cramps, bleeding gums, anaemia, increased infections and slow healing
Food sources: Citrus fruits, blackcurrants, strawberries, kiwi fruit, papaya, red chillies, broccoli, parsley, green leafy veg, peppers
Synergists: Vitamin E, selenium
Inhibitors: Heat, light, oxygen

Nutrient: **Iron**
Function: Essential for healthy red blood cells, oxygen transport, energy production and a healthy immune system
Deficiency signs: Anaemia, fatigue, poor circulation, depression, decreased resistance to infection
Food sources: Red meat, liver, mussels, oysters, chicken, fish, eggs, spinach and green veg, wholemeal bread and fortified breakfast cereal
Synergists: Vitamin C
Inhibitors: Large quantities of tea, calcium supplements, some antacids and anti-gout drugs

Nutrient: **Zinc**
Function: Improves immunity, healing. Needed for healthy eyes, skin, nails for growth and sexual development
Deficiency signs: White spots on nails, loss of taste and appetite, poor growth and wound healing, increased susceptibility to infection, dry flaky skin
Food sources: Oysters, crab and shellfish, other seafood, red meat, chicken, liver, kidney, some green veg, nuts, seeds and wheat germ
Synergists: Vitamin A, Vitamin D, copper
Inhibitors: Alcohol, some diuretics, iron supplements

Not all bacteria are bad. The digestive tract, for example, is the home to our gut flora – millions of different bacteria, many of which are beneficial or 'friendly'. They have a strong hold and act as natural defenders to the body's immune system – preventing unfriendly bacteria taking over.

Everyone's gut flora are different and can change as a result of:

- Stress
- Taking antibiotics: Unfortunately this kills both bad and good bacteria, leaving the gut vulnerable to re-colonisation by harmful bacteria.
- Diarrhoea, which can upset the balance of gut flora
- Irregular meals and poor diets - containing too much fat and alcohol and not enough dietary fibre from fruits and vegetables
- A weak immune system caused by infections such as HIV/Aids, TB and cancer
- Ageing: Unfortunately the good bacteria decrease as we age and we become more vulnerable to infection.
- Food poisoning bacteria causing gastro-enteritis

See *What's a Probiotic,* P. 46

IT'S A FACT:
100,000,000,000,000 bacteria live in the average healthy gut. This mass of bacteria makes up approx 2.2 lbs (1 kg) of our weight.

Variety is the Spice and Elixir of Life: *safe*food tip
Many nutrients are associated with a healthy immune system. Eating a well balanced diet with a variety of foods from each food group is the best way to ensure that we get as many of these immune-boosting nutrients as possible naturally within food. Each food contains a different mix of nutrients, so it is important to include the widest possible variety of foods in our diet.

CANCER DEFENCE BOOSTERS

Every time a cell in our body divides, it must copy the DNA it contains as accurately as possible. However, mistakes are made from time to time – mistakes that can lead to the uncontrolled growth of cancerous cells.

When our immune system is working well, it can spot cancerous cells early on and kill them, but if the immune system is compromised (due to stress or poor nutrition), the risk of developing cancer increases significantly.

It is now estimated that more than 30% of all cancers are related to dietary factors. The health philosophy that prevention is better than cure holds true, particularly for cancer when the treatments can be nearly as distressing as the disease itself.

On a brighter note there is increasing recognition that substances in the diet have real potential to prevent cancer, and this body of evidence continues to grow. There are now more than 200 studies demonstrating the disease-fighting ability of phytochemicals which are found in fruits, vegetables and grains. Scientists continue to identify and explore these powerful phytochemicals and antioxidants which mop up free radicals that cause tissue damage and disease. So far, it remains unclear whether it's an individual phytochemical, or a combination of these plant chemicals that lowers the risk of cancer.

Take prostate cancer as an example. The risk of prostate cancer drops for men who eat tomato products (tomato-based pasta sauces, tomato juice, tomato purees and ketchups). Lycopene, a carotenoid found in tomatoes was thought to be the protective phytochemical. However, studies found that while tomato products significantly reduced the risk of cancer, the same benefit was not apparent from lycopene alone. It appears that tomato-based foods are the key to cancer prevention, not a lycopene supplement. This isn't all that surprising as past experience has taught us that single nutrients or a few nutrients in a supplement do not give the same effect as eating whole foods.

Remember beta-carotene? For years, scientists noted that diets rich in foods containing beta-carotene (carrots and other brightly coloured fruit and vegetables) reduced the risk of many types of cancer, including lung cancer in smokers. But when researchers tested beta-carotene supplements in people who smoked, two major independent studies showed that supplements actually increased the risk of cancer substantially. Beta-carotene supplements also increased the risk of heart attacks and strokes. So it must be something else in carrots and tomatoes that protects us. It could be the effect of hundreds of these phytochemicals and antioxidants working together. But the bottom line is: think 'foods first'.

It is probable that the synergistic effects of phytochemicals in fruit and vegetables are responsible for their potent antioxidant and anticancer activities, and that the benefit of a diet rich in fruit and vegetables is attributed to the complex mixture of phytochemicals present in whole foods.

There's no doubt that we will see novel nutritional approaches to reducing the risk of cancer in the future. Scientific literature is indicating that specific diets and supplements will be available in the future to aid treatment.

What's a phytochemical?

Phytochemicals are plant components that help to keep plants healthy while they're growing. When we eat plant foods, we also benefit from these phytochemicals, which are thought to protect us against disease and boost our immune systems. There are many different types of phytochemicals, including carotenoids, flavonoids and phytoestrogens.

What's a carotenoid?

Carotenoids have antioxidant properties that help keep eyes healthy. Carotenoids are found in the yellow and red pigments of many fruits and vegetables, especially those with deep, rich colours. Lutein and zeaxanthin are especially important for good vision. The optimal amount we need is unknown, but eating at least five servings of fruits and vegetables daily should provide sufficient lutein and zeaxanthin. Great sources include: lutein (spinach, kale, dill, red peppers); zeaxanthin (orange peppers, broccoli, corn, spinach, tangerines and oranges).

What's a flavonoid?

A flavonoid is a type of phytochemical that is found in fruits such as apples, vegetables such as onions, green teas and in wine. It has strong antioxidant properties and may help in the fight against cancers and heart disease.

What's a phytoestrogen?

Phytoestrogens are naturally occurring phenolic compounds found in plant foods. There are two main classes – lignans and isoflavones. Lignans are found in flax seed or linseed, rye, berries, fruits, vegetables and wholegrains. Isoflavones are found in pulses and beans, especially soya beans. Lignans and genistein (a type of isoflavone found in soya beans) have been shown in animal studies to reduce the activity of cancer cells. Further research is required to provide a clearer picture of the effect of dietary phytoestrogens on cancer risk.

What's a probiotic?

The digestive tract is home to our gut flora – millions of different bacteria, many of which are beneficial or 'friendly'. They colonise the gut and act as natural defenders to the body's immune system – preventing unfriendly bacteria taking over. In order to boost the number of friendly bacteria in the gut, many people now eat special probiotic foods and drinks. Probiotics are live bacteria, mostly lactic acid bacteria. They are cultivated and added to foods such as yoghurts and milk drinks. They are also found in certain vitamin and mineral dietary supplements. The bacteria in these foods and supplements need to be robust enough to survive the digestive juices and stomach acid in their journey through the digestive tract. Taking probiotics can help to restore the balance of the gut flora. They also help to improve digestion, irritable bowel syndrome and inflammatory bowel disease. Probiotics increase the uptake of important minerals from the intestine and prevent deficiencies which lower immunity.

FIGHTING CANCER WITH FOODS

Many studies report that vegetarians have fewer instances of cancer that other people. This doesn't mean we should avoid meat – small amounts of lean meat can be part of a healthy diet – but it is probable that vegetarians' high intake of vegetables and fruit helps protect them from disease. The following are guidelines to prompt you to include the foods that science has shown are protective:

- Eat at least five servings of fruit and vegetables a day.

- Eat tomato-based products daily. Men in particular can help to lower their risk of prostate cancer by consuming tomato-based products regularly.

- Use garlic, rosemary and turmeric to season food instead of salt. Early, but as yet inconclusive, studies found that men who ate garlic at least twice a week have a 50% lower risk of prostate cancer than men who never ate garlic. People who eat too much salt double their risk of stomach cancer.

- Drink green tea. Green tea contains epigallocatechin-3-gallate which is thought to cut off the supply of blood to cancer cells.

- Drink alcohol in moderation. The risk of cancer increases with the amount of alcohol consumed and the length of time of over-indulgence.

- Eat fibre-rich foods: wholegrain breakfast cereals and bread, oats, wild rice and beans. Diets low in fibre intake are linked with colon cancer. The more fibre we eat, the less risk we face.

- Eat fewer saturates and more of the protective fats found in oily fish. Certain cancers have been linked with large intakes of saturated fats. People who eat oily fish such as salmon, sardines, tuna and trout twice a week have a significantly reduced risk of colon cancer.

- Maintain a healthy weight. Being the correct weight for your height is important. Being even slightly too heavy increases the risk of a range of cancers.

Use turmeric and ginger in cooking. Ginger has been used for hundreds of years to prevent or treat nausea and now some scientists believe that the plant can also help people with cancer avoid the nausea induced by chemotherapy. Curcumin, the yellow pigment in the spice turmeric has been found to inhibit melanoma cell growth and kill tumour cells. Early, but as yet inconclusive, studies have linked high consumption of turmeric to lower rates of breast cancer, prostate cancer, lung cancer and colon cancer.

Drink green tea: It is good for additional flavonoids and antioxidants

Limit alcoholic drinks to one a day or less.
Asian women who have traditionally eaten soya have a lower risk of breast cancer. Scientists have suggested that this is due to compounds in soya known as *phytoestrogens*. Many studies have looked at the effect of soya consumption on breast cancer risk in recent years. The evidence is indicating that there is strong protective effect if women consume soya from adolescence through adulthood. This strongly points to the benefit of consuming soya throughout life. However, the science is far from conclusive and there is still a question mark over whether breast cancer patients should start consuming soya products when they have not been part of their diet throughout life. Many women have looked towards phytoestrogen supplements, but to date there have not been enough safety tests done, and to date little evidence to show that they have the same effect as soya foods. What is clear is that soya food has been proven scientifically to reduce cholesterol levels and there is emerging evidence demonstrating that they are beneficial for bone health too.

MANAGING THE MENOPAUSE

Nature can be cruel. Not only does a women have to go through the 'change of life' when she's half a century old, she may also experience menstrual irregularities, hot flushes and irritability anywhere between five and ten years beforehand. And there's more: after this major milestone in life, she faces a decline in bone mass and an increased risk of heart disease!

Luckily, many women sail through the menopause hardly noticing it has happened. Others however can be distressed to varying degrees by unpleasant symptoms of hot flushes, night sweats, mood swings and memory problems. These symptoms are caused by the lack of the female hormone, oestrogen, which the ovaries stop producing around the age of fifty. Some women opt for hormone replacement therapy to provide relief from their menopausal symptoms. However, recent scientific studies raised concerns about how long-term therapy can increase the risk of breast cancer, so more women are now motivated to look out for alternatives. Maybe it's simply a belief that nature should take its own course. As those with a family history of breast cancer are at a higher risk, any concerns will be addressed at an individual medical assessment.

Japanese women report suffering more rarely from menopausal symptoms perhaps because of their high intake of phytoestrogens. The major dietary sources of phytoestrogens (in particular isoflavones) are soya beans, tofu, soya bean flour, soya milk and linseed. Although these phytoestrogens are much weaker than the real oestrogen women's bodies produce, they can bond to oestrogen receptors in the body and in its absence have just enough of an effect to put a damper on those uncomfortable symptoms. Soya also reduces cholesterol absorption from the gut and increases cholesterol excretion. The overall benefit is the lowering of LDL (bad) cholesterol by up to 30% and a simultaneous increase in HDL (good) cholesterol by up to 15%.

The following foods contain approximately 50mg of Isoflavones

100g firm tofu
200g soft tofu
100g miso
250ml soya milk or soya yoghurt
50g soya flour, cooked soya beans or TVP

Most studies that have looked at the effect of soya foods and supplements on menopausal symptoms such as hot flushes and night sweats have found no significant effect. However, some anecdotal evidence has suggested that while variable, they can be effective for some women.

Asian women eat between 25 and 200mg of isoflavone-rich soya every day. At this point in time we don't know enough about isoflavones to recommend a daily amount that we should eat, but it appears that an intake of 50-120mg of isoflavones a day has some therapeutic effects. On average this can be provided by one or two portions of soya products a day.

The role of calcium in preventing bone mineral loss during the menopause has been studied extensively. Calcium supplementation doesn't seem to have any major effect on bone density at the time of the menopause. However, calcium supplementation seems to slow bone-loss in women five years post-menopause. More research is needed in this area. At present it's advisable to include a range of calcium-rich foods in the diet to ensure optimal intake. Some of the best sources of calcium are dairy products, including milk, cheese, yoghurts and dairy-based desserts. Other sources include canned fish (including bones), bread and cereal foods, pulses, some green vegetables (broccoli and spinach) and some nuts and seeds (sesame seeds and peanuts). Exposing the face and arms to sunlight results in the manufacture of vitamin D, which is critical for the absorption of calcium. Dietary sources of vitamin D include fortified spreads, meat and meat products and oily fish (salmon and mackerel).

At the menopause, when periods stop, the iron requirements of women are reduced to the same level as men. Even though iron requirements are not as high in post-menopausal women, it is still important to include a range of iron-containing foods in the diet. Lean red meat, poultry and fish are the best sources of iron. Iron is also found in pulses, nuts, dark green vegetables and dried fruit, but is less well absorbed from these sources. Vitamin C containing foods such as fresh orange juice, salad or green vegetables can help absorption of iron from these plant foods.

Although the menopause is a change in life, there's no reason why it can't be a change for the better. More and more women are living longer and healthier lives, contributing significantly to our work force and family lives. Variety and balance are the cornerstones of a good diet and many women are living evidence that life begins at fifty!

We are advised to eat at least five portions of fruit and vegetables a day but what exactly is a portion? *safe*food clarifies:

- 2 small fruits, e.g. plums, kiwis, mandarins
- 1 medium fruit, e.g. apple, pear, banana
- 1 slice of a large fruit, e.g. melon, pineapple
- A handful of grapes, berries or cherries
- 1 heaped tablespoon of dried fruits, e.g. raisins
- 1 glass of fruit juice (fruit juice should only contribute to one portion a day even if you have more than one glass in a day, as you are not getting any fibre in the juice and the sugars are concentrated)
- 2–3 heaped tablespoons of vegetables
- Dessert bowl of salad
- 3 heaped tablespoons of beans or pulses

HEART HEALTH

Why should we check our cholesterol and blood pressure regularly?

- Too much cholesterol on the walls of our arteries forms a plaque.
- The plaque narrows the space for the blood to run through and restricts its flow.
- The heart has to pump harder to get blood through these narrow arteries.
- This can result in high blood pressure.
- Sometimes bits of the plaque can rupture and break off, causing a complete block inside an artery supplying blood to the heart or to the brain.
- This can result in a heart attack or stroke.

Each risk factor below speeds up the development of plaque on the inside walls of arteries and puts you at greater risk of a heart attack:

✓ Very overweight or obese
✓ High blood cholesterol
✓ High blood pressure
✓ High blood glucose levels
✓ Low levels of physical activity
✓ Diabetes
✓ Smoking

Cholesterol is a fatty substance found in every cell in the body. It is mainly produced by the liver but the way we eat and the type of fat we eat also affect the level of cholesterol in the blood. Fried and fast foods, cakes, biscuits, pastries, fatty snack foods, fatty meats, cream, butter and hard cheeses are generally high in saturated fats and/or trans fats. Too much saturated fat or trans fat can raise Low Density Lipoproteins (LDL: bad cholesterol).

For a healthier heart and weight you need to swing the balance in favour of more fresh foods, fruits and vegetables, wholegrain and oat-based cereals, low fat dairy products, nuts and seeds, oily fish and lean meat. Buy a spread that is higher in monounsaturated fat.

Positive choices for a healthier heart

CEREAL FOODS (ESPECIALLY OAT-BASED FOODS)

Wholegrain and oat-based cereals include unsweetened muesli and porridge, wholegrain nutty breads, wholemeal pasta, brown rice and jacket potatoes. These foods contain a combination of insoluble fibre and soluble fibre. Four out of five people need to increase their intake of fibre. Have a bowl of cereal in the morning, two slices of wholegrain bread for lunch and an average serving of pasta, rice or potato for dinner. Soluble fibre, found in wholegrains (oats, in particular), forms a gel in the intestine that causes the elimination of bile acids from the liver before they can be absorbed. In response, the liver uses cholesterol to form bile salts, thereby reducing the amount of blood cholesterol.

FRUITS AND VEGETABLES (ESPECIALLY FRESH)

This includes any kind of fresh or frozen fruits and vegetables (frozen veg is just as nutritious as fresh), juices and smoothies. These foods are packed with antioxidants and folate. Eat a minimum of five portions of fruit and vegetables a day. Drink a glass of juice or smoothie to supplement your intake. Fruit and vegetables contain protective antioxidant vitamins which mop up damaging free radicals and stop the oxidation of bad LDL cholesterol.

NUTS (ESPECIALLY BRAZIL NUTS)

Nuts are very high in calories so have a handful two or three times a week in salads, breads or cereal. Nuts are excellent alternative sources of protein, are low in saturated fats and high in the essential fats. They contain potent antioxidants, Vitamin E and selenium. Brazil nuts are particularly high in selenium. Walnuts, peanuts and hazelnuts are especially rich in essential fats. Choose unsalted varieties.

PEAS, BEANS (ESPECIALLY SOYA BEANS) AND LENTILS

Replacing some of the meat in your diet three or four times a week with peas, beans and lentils can help reduce your total fat and saturated fat and boost your intake of nutrients. Some of these foods are: chickpea products such as hummus, soya bean products such as tofu, baked beans, bean salads, lentil soups and garden peas. All of these are excellent sources of protein and are low in saturated fats. They contain small amounts of the better types of fats, poly- and monounsaturates, which are better for blood cholesterol.

FISH (ESPECIALLY OILY FISH)

One to two portions of oily fish (salmon, herring, mackerel) and one white (cod or plaice) per week is recommended. Oily fish contains omega 3 fat: a type of polyunsaturated fat which reduces the tendency for blood to clot and lowers the risk of heart attack.

MEAT

Too much red meat can raise your intake of bad fats (saturates), but in moderation lean red meat (such as beef, pork, ham [trimmed of fat], venison, chicken and turkey) is an excellent source of protein, Vitamin B12, zinc and iron. Ideally, eat a medium portion (90g) three to four times a week.

EGGS

Eggs and functional eggs (those containing omega 3 fats and vitamin E resulting from hens' enriched diet) are a good source of protein and fat soluble vitamins A, D and E. Limit yourself to three ordinary eggs or six functional eggs per week.

MILK, CHEESE AND YOGHURT

Calcium-rich foods like the following are vital for your bones: low fat milk and yoghurts, lower fat cheeses such as brie, camembert, gouda, reduced fat cheddar, edam, cottage. Have a glass of low fat milk over cereal or as a drink, a low fat yoghurt and a matchbox size portion of cheese every day. Low fat dairy foods are lower in saturated fat and are rich in calcium which is vital in controlling blood pressure.

FATS AND OILS

Both total cholesterol and bad LDL cholesterol are lowered when saturated fats (butter, fats in biscuits etc) are replaced with monounsaturated fat (olive oil, nuts, olive oil spreads). Use spray-on monounsaturated oil for stir-fries, and rapeseed or olive oil for salad dressings; we use less when we spray on instead of pouring. Use all fats and oils sparingly and avoid using spread on bread and potatoes, especially when they have another filling or topping.

DRINKS

Green tea or ordinary tea, mineral, spring or filtered tap water, unsweetened fruit juice and red wine are all good, heart-friendly choices. It is recommended to drink approximately 11 glasses of fluid a day, mainly as water and tea. Tea contains a number of flavonoids, which are potent antioxidants and help reduce the risk of blood clots in the arteries. Up to 14 units of alcohol for women and 21 units for men per week is the recommended intake. Moderate consumption of alcohol is beneficial to heart health, and the benefits are partly due to its effect on raising good HDL cholesterol.

SALT, SAUCES AND DRESSINGS

Garlic, herbs, spices, lemon juice, black pepper, low fat vinaigrettes, and sauces with less than 3% fat should be used instead of salt, soya sauce, creamy sauces and salad dressings. Garlic can add flavour to foods and reduce the need for salt. It also contains allicin, which may help to keep the blood thin, and help to lower the bad LDL cholesterol and blood pressure levels.

CAKES, BISCUITS, SWEETS AND TREATS

Options such as oat-based biscuits, fruitcake, carrot cake or brack are better than those which contain cream, chocolate, sugar and fat. Just enjoy in moderate amounts, occasionally. If you are really battling with weight, 'treat' foods are the first targets for reduction. Many shop-bought cakes, biscuits and crackers contain trans-fatty acids which cause a rise in total and bad LDL cholesterol.

The *North South Ireland Food Consumption Survey* found that biscuits, cakes, confectionary and savoury snacks account for one fifth of adults' saturated fat intake. The *National Children's Food Survey* showed that among children aged 5–12 years, these foods account for a staggering one fifth of total calorie and fat intake

***safe*food recommends that we keep foods such as biscuits, cakes, chocolate and crisps as treats. They are readily available and tempt us throughout the day, but provide us only with lots of calories, fat, sugar or salt and very few vitamins and minerals.**

Choose no more than one of these treats each day:

- **One snack or mini-size chocolate bar – not regular or supersizes**
- **One 25g bag of crisps, not a 40g bag**
- **Cut down from three biscuits at a time to two**
- **Share a slice of cake or pudding with somebody else**

Fat Facts

We need to eat a certain amount and type of fat for our bodies to function properly. For example, our bodies can't make essential fatty acids, so we need to eat them.

Fat provides us with fat soluble vitamins A, D and E.

Fat is a more concentrated source of calories than carbohydrate or protein, providing 9 calories in every gram; carbohydrate and protein provide just 4 calories in a gram.

Eating too much total fat, whatever the type, can therefore help us to gain weight and become obese, unless we burn off these calories.

Eating the wrong type of fat also causes problems, and by increasing harmful blood cholesterol levels can lead to coronary heart disease. We have two main types of cholesterol in the body: HDL cholesterol and LDL cholesterol.

High Density Lipoprotein (HDL)

This is healthy cholesterol: it mops up cholesterol left behind in arteries and gets rid of it from the body. Regular physical exercise increases the level of HDL cholesterol in the body and keeps the heart healthy.

Low Density Lipoprotein (LDL)

This is bad cholesterol because it sticks to the walls in the arteries, causing them to narrow. This reduces the blood supply to the heart or brain which can lead to heart disease and stroke. It's important to maintain a low level of LDL cholesterol because high levels are a risk factor of heart disease.

Eating too much saturated fat and trans fat can increase harmful LDL cholesterol.

Replacing some saturated fat with monounsaturated fats such as olive oil and polyunsaturated fat such as omega 3 fish oils can help to lower harmful LDL cholesterol and the risk of heart disease.

How much fat is enough?

The table below highlights the recommended daily intake of fats in the diet for average men and women which should be used as a guideline to the total fat eaten in a day.

Guideline daily amounts

Each Day	Women	Men
Calories	2000	2500
Fat	70g	95g
Salt	5g	7g
Omega 3 (RDA FSAI)	10g	12.5g

Other Fats

Trans Fatty Acids

These fats are formed during the factory process of partial hydrogenation, where a liquid oil is turned into a spreadable fat. Some are also found naturally in foods, but most trans fatty acids in the diet come from hydrogenated fat. Trans fatty acids increase the risk of heart disease and for this reason the intake of these fats from all sources should be kept low. Sources include spreads and margarines, crackers, biscuits and frozen pizzas.

Plant Sterols and Stanols

Plant sterols are present naturally in small quantities in many fruits, vegetables, nuts, seeds, cereals, legumes (peas, beans and lentils), vegetable oils and other plant sources. Plant stanols occur in even smaller quantities in many of the same sources. Both stanols and sterols are essential components of plant cell membranes and structurally resemble cholesterol. They can block the level of absorption of cholesterol in the gut when a sufficient amount is eaten. As a result, less cholesterol passes into the bloodstream and more cholesterol passes out of the body. Functional dairy spreads containing these plant sterols and stanols are now available, and these help to reduce the levels of blood cholesterol in the body by 10% when used as part of a healthy diet.

Fatty acids are saturated, monounsaturated, or polyunsaturated.

Two types of polyunsaturated fatty acid exist: the omega 6 and the omega 3 fatty acids. The omega 6 fatty acids are available mainly from vegetable oils. Three types of omega 3 fatty acids exist: (alpha) linolenic acid is available from certain plants but eicosapentanoic acid and docosahexanoic acid must be obtained from marine sources.

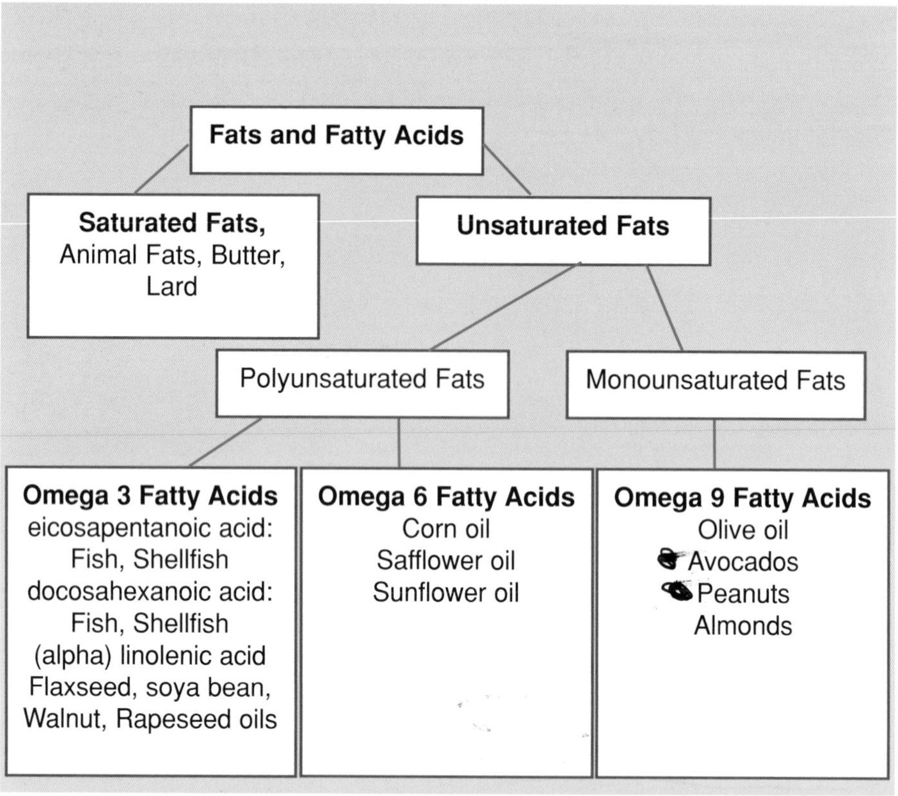

SALT BELONGS IN THE SEA, NOT IN YOUR FOOD!

Sodium or salt is required in very small amounts by our bodies to regulate our fluid balance and to transmit nerve impulses.

Eating too much salt can cause our blood pressure to rise and increase the risk of stroke, heart disease and kidney failure.

The good news is that by becoming more aware of hidden salt and reducing our intake by about 3–4g per day, we can significantly reduce our risk of these diseases.

FOOD SOURCES OF SALT

It's obvious that some foods,such as nuts and crisps, have lots of added salt. However many everyday foods, such as bread, breakfast cereals and biscuits, contain quite a lot of 'hidden' salt, and it can be difficult to find low salt alternatives.

Cured and processed meats such as bacon, ham, sausage, canned soups and vegetables can contain considerable amounts of added salt depending upon the required flavour. Salt is also added to processed food to act as a preservative.

On a food label it may be listed in the ingredients list in different ways. For example as: Salt; sodium; monosodium glutamate (MSG); sodium nitrite; baking soda (sodium bicarbonate).

TIPS ON REDUCING SALT INTAKE

The most obvious way to cut down on salt is to use less when cooking or at the table. The advice here is to take the salt cellar off the table and to use pepper and other fresh herbs and spices to flavour food. Healthier alternatives to salt include lemon juice, garlic and pepper.

***safe*food tip**

Even if we completely stopped adding salt to our food, we would still be 100% over the recommended daily allowance. How? Because between 65% and 70% of the salt that we eat comes from processed food, and canteen and restaurant food. A small amount of salt, about 4 grams a day, is essential to health. At most we should eat 6 grams, or 1 teaspoon. But be very careful – this includes all the salt you eat in processed foods as well as what you add yourself.

*safe***food**'s market research uncovered the behaviours and attitudes of Irish people towards salt. 91% of people on the island of Ireland are aware that salt is bad for their health, with 49% associating it with high blood pressure. However, one-third of the Irish population do not know what their RDA of salt is. Furthermore, of the people who season their food when cooking, nearly 50% do so without tasting it.

Cut down on the amount of processed foods you buy and foods which are known to be high in salt e.g. bacon, smoked fish, stock cubes, gravy, soya sauce, crackers, crisps and salted nuts.

Fresh meats such as beef, pork, lamb and chicken are all naturally low in salt, but be careful of the packets and jars of sauce you use, which may substantially increase the salt content.

Check the claim and the label. If a food claims to be 'low salt', it should contain no more than 0.3g salt per 100g (this is equivalent to 0.12g sodium per 100g).

BONE FOODS

How many of us really perceive ourselves to be personally at risk of bone disease? We tend to think we will have plenty of time to worry about our heart and bones when we reach fifty or sixty! Wrong! The critical time to think about bone health is now, whatever age you are. Every single day counts, particularly in the early years.

Bones are metabolically very active, constantly being worn away and rebuilt. In fact our entire skeleton is replaced about once every ten years. Rebuilding is essential because the forces transmitted through the bones when we walk, run or jump cause tiny stress fractures. We need this stress to keep bone stimulated to produce more bone tissue, and we need nutrients to ensure the bone we build up is healthy.

In healthy young people, bone growth is faster than bone loss. Their bones grow and strengthen through the first twenty years of life.

During our thirties and forties, bone loss and bone regeneration are in balance so there is little change.

Unfortunately it's downhill after that. After fifty, bone regeneration slows down, but we still lose bone at the same pace – so this results in a progressive loss of bone.

There are many factors that influence bone health. Bone disease is linked to factors such as a lack of oestrogen, low body weight and lifestyle factors such as inactivity, smoking and drinking too much alcohol.

Bone Foods

Calcium	Milk, cheese, yogurt, seaweeds, canned fish, nuts and seeds
Vitamin D	Oily fish and fish liver oil supplements, egg yolk, liver and fortified breakfast cereals
Magnesium	Wheat bran, nuts, seeds, seaweeds and hummus
Phosphorous	Yeast extract, wheatgerm and bran, nuts, seeds, seaweeds and cheese

High protein and high salt diets are known to increase bone loss.

The calcium found in milk and dairy products is easily absorbed. This mineral however is less available from plant foods. Sometimes foods such as wholegrain cereals and pulses, which contain phytates, and spinach and rhubarb, which contain oxalates, make calcium difficult to absorb by the body. Many soya products, such as tofu and soya drinks, are fortified with calcium and so can be a useful source of calcium for vegans.

Vitamin D is also important for healthy bones because it helps us absorb calcium from food. Vitamin D is made in skin that is exposed to sunlight. Some of us who wear UV protection, who are housebound or who wear clothes that cover most of the body, need to be sure we get adequate Vitamin D. Few foods contain large quantities of this vitamin. Fish liver oils have very high levels, and oily fish, eg sardines and tuna, are also rich sources.

Check out your calcium intake

Children, adults and older people need 800mg of calcium every day. Adolescents, pregnant and nursing women need 1200mg of calcium every day.

Each of the following foods provides approximately 200mg of calcium. How many do you get in an average day?

- **A glass of milk (whole, low fat or skimmed milk)**
- **Half a glass of fortified milk (with added calcium)**
- **A small glass of orange juice with added calcium**
- **A glass of goats' milk**
- **A glass of soya milk with added calcium**
- **Two and a half litres of mineral water**
- **30g Cheddar, Edam or Emmenthal cheese. An average cheese sandwich is made with 60g of cheese**
- **60g Camembert cheese**
- **45g Brie cheese**
- **300g Cottage cheese**
- **A medium portion of Tofu with added calcium**
- **4 fromage frais**
- **3 fortified fromage frais (with added calcium)**
- **3 scoops of ice cream**

- **1 cheeseburger**
- **1 slice (70g) cheese pizza**
- **1 portion (420g) of lasagne**
- **40g tinned sardines (softened bones contain the calcium)**
- **250g tinned salmon (softened bones contain the calcium). A small tin of salmon weighs 105g and a large tin weighs 213g**
- **8 thin slices (210g) of white bread**
- **3 (150g) crusty white rolls (each roll is roughly the size of one-third of a baguette)**
- **7 large helpings (630g) of cabbage**
- **7 servings (490g) of broccoli**
- **3 tablespoons(30g) sesame seeds**

Spinach has some calcium but it is not easily absorbed by the body and for this reason it is not listed as a possible source of calcium

When slimming, don't cut out dairy

It's worrying that the last National Nutrition Survey (in 2001) found that almost one in four Irish women were not getting enough calcium in their diets. In addition, there seems to be an increasing number of women buying weight-loss books and following weight-loss programmes which exclude dairy foods, many of which are based on pseudo science. Milk, cheese and yoghurt combined provide 48% of calcium in the Irish diet. The next most important source is bread which provides 17% of calcium. People may lose the weight on a fad diet in the short term, but there are hidden side effects and women will be really challenged to meet their calcium needs without dairy products.

Numerous studies in the last three years have investigated the link between calcium and obesity. Many have shown that calcium could significantly enhance weight and fat loss in obese people already following a low-calorie diet. Scientists have not yet uncovered the mechanism behind this effect but research continues. One hypothesis suggests that it has to do with the actions of Vitamin D or calcitrol. Calcitrol causes fat cells to create more fat and its levels are raised if the diet is low in calcium. By contrast, high-calcium diets suppress calcitrol and, as a consequence, promote the burning of fat. If you want to slim effectively, it seems critical to include three servings of low fat dairy foods not just for bone health, but also for the waistline.

***safe*food** recommends low fat versions of dairy foods. One easy switch to make in the home is to buy low fat milk. Anybody over the age of two can drink low fat milk. Full fat milk is best for toddlers under the age of two, so buy full fat milk for them and choose low fat milk for the rest of the family.

When there are insufficient levels of magnesium and calcium in the blood, the body pulls them from your bones, increasing the risk of osteoporosis.

Additives

A recent study looked at the association between food additives (colours and preservatives) and behavioural problems in children. It was conducted on a sample of three-year-old children over a two year period. Parents reported an improvement in their children's behaviour when the additives were removed from their diets. More extensive research on the effects of certain additives and preservatives on behaviour have been commissioned by the Food Standards Authority in the UK. Watch this space. In the meantime limit sweets and drinks with lots of colours and preservatives.

A super-sized fast food meal (large burger, fries, dessert and soft drink) can contain as much as 2,200 calories, which would mean you would need to run the equivalent of a marathon (26 miles) to burn it off!

In this section you will find a road map to a healthier life. It is not a difficult journey and is one you should enjoy. It helps to clearly define your goals and plan your daily routines. It has taken years to shape the body you have and it may take time to re-shape it, so be patient.

A little aerobic conditioning, some strength training and stretches will help condition, de-stress and enhance your lifestyle.

By opening these pages, you have taken the first step towards a more positive and rewarding lifestyle. So bear with me, because the only muscles I am asking you to exercise at the moment are those of your eyes; the tears [redacted]

If the word ‘exercise’ generates great fear and trepidation and conjures up an image of pain and no gain, the good news is that it’s not about around-the-clock training or arriving home and collapsing into the chair with exhaustion. Exercise should be about preventing heart failure, not causing it.

Don’t fall into the trap of thinking, ‘I run up and down a ladder all day’ or ‘I have to walk up that corridor every day, therefore I exercise every day’. This kind of activity is often stress-related and not enough to help us to get fit. We need to put the time aside for some exercise and get rid of the stresses of the day. In a short time we will reap the rewards.

The great interest in exercise and wellbeing today is the result of many factors, one of them being the growing awareness of obesity. The benefits of exercise are innumerable, affecting every single cell and organ in the body. It also affects hormone secretion which can regulate everything from diabetes and weight gain to your mood. It affects how you walk, talk, breathe, think, move and feel. There is no getting away from it: body, mind and soul exercise is good for you! And it’s never too late to start.

Prioritise, don’t become a statistic. Since 1990, obesity has increased in Ireland by 67%. If this continues, three-quarters of our population will be overweight in the next ten to fifteen years. Obesity is costing the Irish economy at least 340 million euro annually.

Obesity, along with cardio-vascular disease and diabetes, is set to push annual deaths from 2.5 million per year to 5 million by 2020. Cancer deaths are set to increase to 15 million new cases by 2020. This 50% increase is due to an ageing population, current trends in smoking and inactivity.

Looking at these statistics, we must ask: what are the barriers to healthy living in this country? After thirteen years in the industry I have heard all the excuses: kids, work, tiredness. We put exercise at the end of our priority list. Believe it or not, to create energy we have to use energy. It’s not hard to be healthy and energetic and to feel good, it’s just a choice. Exercise is a key ingredient in illness and disease prevention. *Get active!* Exercise is the medical prescription for healthy living in the twenty-first century.

Let us help you break down these barriers to healthy living. I invite you to start exercising and follow the simple life-changing principles of this book for a guaranteed result in helping you to achieve your goals. You owe it to yourself and those you love. Many people fail to start an exercise programme because they don’t have the information to help guide them. Welcome to the road map to a healthier lifestyle.

10 REASONS TO START EXERCISING

1. Improve Long Term Health and Wellbeing

Studies show how a small amount of exercise done regularly can drastically improve your health and wellbeing. Just once or twice a week is sufficient to reduce your chances of developing serious disease, while helping to control total cholesterol levels. It also improves your quality of life as you age.

2. Increase Energy

To create energy we have to use energy. You may feel a little tired before you commence an exercise routine, but I guarantee that once you start, you will be full of energy and asking yourself why you were feeling so tired. Physical activity helps you work, rest and play.

3. Increase Metabolism and Help Maintain Muscle

The real goal of burning calories is not to burn them during activity, but at rest, when healthy eating and activity increases the body's ability to burn them. Through exercise, we increase our metabolism (the rate at which our bodies maintain normal function). The more muscle we maintain, the higher our metabolism rises. This results in decreased body fat, reduced weight and a tighter, fitter-looking body.

4. Increase Bone Density

Peak bone mass tends to be reached at thirty years of age and declines thereafter. Activity helps maintain and increase bone density while increasing joint stability. Performing specific exercises helps to balance muscle groups leading, to more strength and better posture. The result is looking confident and feeling a lot better.

5. Decrease Stress and Anxiety

Exercise helps release endorphins, which are our natural pain blockers, while increasing alpha waves in the brain. Alpha waves are electrical patterns of brain activity which indicate that the mind is more relaxed, helping to relieve tension and creating a euphoric state. You probably won't jump around with joy after your first exercise session – it takes time for the body to recognise new activity – but stick with it and the benefits will come.

6. Combat Signs of Ageing

Exercise will help you feel younger, look better and function more effectively.

7. Improve Sex Life

Exercise stimulates the endocrine glands, resulting in a heightened sex drive and desire.

8. Increase Flexibilty

Regular stretching can release tension in tired muscles, balance muscle groups and decrease risk of injury. Stretching also increases your energy as flexible joints require less energy to complete daily tasks.

9. Improve Co-Ordination

Exercise helps improve co-ordination and motor skills.

10. Help aid Childbirth, and Speed up Recovery Post Birth

Regular exercise before, during and after pregnancy can provide a mother with a far greater level of physical strength to carry and deliver a child. It will also provide strength to help with breast feeding and lifting the baby and buggy. It also helps to create a positive attitude and body image for the new mother.

Exercise

Improves Long Term Health and Wellbeing
Increases Energy
Increases Metabolism and helps Maintain Muscle
Increases Bone Density, Strengthens and Improves Posture
Decreases Stress and Anxiety
Combats Signs of Ageing
Improves your Sex Life
Increases Flexibility
Improves Co-Ordination
Helps aid Childbirth and Speeds up Recovery Post Birth

Fact and Fantasy

Myth: All strength exercise will turn you into Arnold Schwarzenegger.

Truth: What determines the result of your training is the exercise selection and programme design. If you want to look like Arnold, train specifically for it. If you want to look like a fashion model, you can train for that too.

Myth: Muscle turns to fat or flab.

Truth: If we have lean muscle on the body and higher energy expenditure due to activity, we burn more calories while at rest. We fuel this energy output with dietary intake. If we suddenly stop, muscle will waste away to nothing within 72 hours of non-use, resulting in loss of strength within 10 days. With this muscle loss our energy output drops, so we burn fewer calories. With more time on our hands, we tend to eat more and weight goes on, but it's not muscle that turns to fat or flab.

Myth: Exercise makes you musclebound.

Truth: If you train with an incorrect technique or don't stretch properly, you may find you end up with restricted movement, but exercise done correctly will improve your range of motion.

Myth: You must stretch prior to exercise.

Truth: Prior to exercise, we need to warm up, not stretch. Warming up means increasing heart rate and body temperature. If we stop and stretch we end up cooling back down. The important time to stretch is at the end of training, not before (see *Flexibility and Stretching* section).

Myth: You must breathe out on effort.

Truth: Holding the breath for a long period of time is not good for you. Some exercises involve holding the breath, but only for a moment. There is a right time for breathing, sometimes on effort, sometimes not. The best way to remember is whenever the chest lifts, breathe in: not only do the lungs expand, but it also helps to stabilise the spine.

Myth: Strength training increases blood pressure.

Truth: If blood pressure increases, it is usually due to steroids, overtraining or a diet that is too high in fat. Studies now seem to show exercise can help to reduce blood pressure.

Before You Start an Exercise Programme

HEALTH SCREEN

If you have particular cardiovascular risk factors, you should discuss your proposed training regime with your GP. If, at any age, you answer yes to any of the following questions, make an appointment.

1. Have you been told you have a heart condition? Do you take blood pressure or heart medication?
2. Do you feel pain or discomfort in your chest when you do physical activity?
3. Do you ever become dizzy or lose consciousness?
4. Do you have bone or joint problems that may inflame during activity?
5. Are you a diabetic?
6. Are you on any medication?
7. Are you pregnant or post pregnant?

GOALS, TIME AND CONSISTENCY

Decide what is the purpose of your exercise programme and what you want to achieve. Be realistic with the time you allocate to your training, taking into account family, work and other commitments. Don't fool yourself by planning four sessions a week, when three is more practical. A gym 25 miles away is unlikely to be used.

Many people coming from a sedentary occupation try to train seven days a week and are doomed to fail. Be realistic about weight loss and set your mind to a consistent number of hours a week to kick the metabolism into action. A sluggish system is slow to burn calories.

It is far better to be consistent than a weekend warrior. Exercise hormones and endorphins are natural pain blockers. To get the feelgood factor of exercise, the body needs to be pushed a little so it recognises it is being exercised. This won't happen overnight but by starting training slowly, the intensity can be built up gradually, without causing injury.

The best route to staying consistent and preventing failure is to plan your training a week in advance. When you have an idea of next week's schedule, add training days and times to the diary. This way, even if it's raining, you know you should still go for the planned walk, or fit in a gym session after work or during lunchbreak. Television programmes should not be allowed to interfere with plans, or should be factored into the timetable.

Footwear

WHEN PURCHASING A SHOE:

- Choosing the right footwear will protect against the jarring actions of exercise activities. Buy the shoe to suit your planned activity: a runner needs running shoes; a walker, walking shoes; and there are cross-trainers for those who want to combine several activities.
- Choose a reputable shoe or sports store with a large inventory.
- Don't just assume your normal shoe size will be the same as for runners, get fitted for each pair.
- If you have a high arch you will require greater shock absorbency as you may be prone to ankle sprains and instability.
- Low arches will require greater support and heel control.

As most shoes lose their cushioning after about six months of regular use, be practical and avoid paying out more money than you need to.

BUDDY TRAINING

Try to influence a friend to train with you. It's great motivation and can make your choice of activity more fun. However, remember the buddy system is about training and not arriving at your mate's house and sitting down for coffee. Coffee will dehydrate you before you start and you will slow down too much and lose motivation. Arrive dressed and ready to go.

Exercise choices – all good for fitness

Walking	Running
Cycling	Swimming
Weight Training	Studio Classes
Hill Walking	Rock Climbing, Abseiling
Dance	Skipping
Tennis/Racquet sport	Handball
Boxing	Martial Arts
Golf	

POSTURE

Good posture makes us look and feel better and we need to practise it. With the chest tall we immediately ease the back and look smarter and more professional.

It is easy to develop rounded shoulders when we don't sit up straight. One of the worst problems of poor posture manifests itself in forward head positioning.

wrong

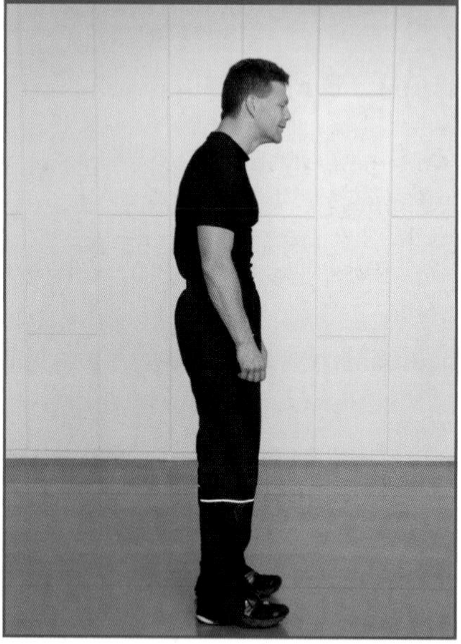

right

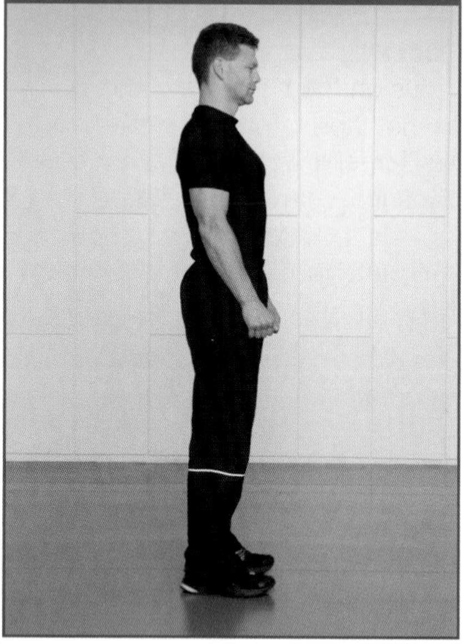

We have seven vertebrae in the neck supporting the head. They are mobile, forming a curved shape. If we develop forward head positioning, which is not always visible to the eye, these bones stiffen and lose their curvature. As a result, the upper neck muscles shorten and tighten, we get an increase in the curvature of the mid back or thoracic region, and the muscles of this region weaken and lengthen. As the head is heavy, the muscles are too weak to correct the rounded shoulder syndrome and, without being aware of the danger of jutting the head forward, damage can be done to the neck and back, causing pain and restricted movement.

Check yourself. Driving the car, do your upper back and head contact with the upper seat and headrest? Do you thrust your head forward while working at a computer, or even at home eating, watching television? Some even develop forward head positioning while walking.

Most likely to develop forward head position:

- People who drive a lot
- People who spend long periods of time sitting at a desk or in front of a computer or TV
- Women who are pregnant, because of the change in their centre of gravity
- Breast-feeding mums
- People who train their chest muscles and don't balance it with back training, or do too many press-ups
- People working long hours have muscle fatigue
- Those who are on their feet all day, or don't get enough sleep.

It seems we are all prone!

Correcting Posture

Focus on the lift of the chest, relax the shoulders, arms and head as if they are not there. You will immediately feel the head coming into a better position, the tummy tightens, the shoulders drop down and back, putting less pressure on the spine. Take your time, get it right and practise. Don't lift the shoulders as you take a deep breath in, as this will create more tension. Don't squeeze your shoulder blades together, the muscles will tire. Don't push the head back. It is a skeletal correction.

Once you can do it seated, try it standing. Stand as you normally would. Throw the head and shoulders off to the side, lifting the chest, pushing from the mid back, don't exaggerate the movement. Don't push your hips forward, just lift the chest. When standing with correct posture, we can feel the tummy tighten, which helps give a little more protection to the lower back.

A good place to practice is in the car, sitting in traffic. Get into the habit of doing it at every set of traffic lights. Try it when sitting, eating dinner, out walking and after a while it will become natural. Remember, when lifting, don't 'chin', especially when lifting (a child for example) from below. It is easy to throw the chin forward, so keep the chest tall, even when bending.

Water and Exercise

With or without exercise, water is essential. It must be consumed from the start of the day to the end, not in one sitting. For optimal performance, fluids must be drunk before, during and after exercise. This enables the protection facilities to work properly and the muscles to burn calories more efficiently.

It's not about any fluid intake: tea, soft drinks and alcohol are not of benefit and tend to dehydrate you. Water is best for rehydration. Apart from thirst, if you find you suffer from muscle cramps, dizziness, lack of concentration, blurred vision, nausea, a lot of injuries and delays in recovery, look at the amount of water you have drunk during exercise, you may need more.

THE BIG PICTURE OF FITNESS

There are four components to any fitness or exercise routine. If we lack any of these, we under-achieve and miss out on all-round improvements in our health.

1. Aerobic Exercise, e.g. walking/running, heart and lung fitness
2. Strength Training, e.g. weight training, muscular development
3. Flexibility, e.g. to stretch, mobilise joints and lengthen muscles
4. Water

Aerobic Training is often thought of activity done in leotards, Strength Training as generating bulging muscles, and Flexibility nothing more than a good stretch while brushing teeth. These are myths and excuses for avoiding exercise.

AEROBIC TRAINING – CARDIO RESPIRATORY FITNESS

Aerobic fitness best describes the health and function of the heart, lungs and the circulatory system these serve, and relates to the ability of the person to sustain an activity for prolonged periods without undue fatigue. Energy is derived aerobically when oxygen is utilised to metabolise food and to deliver energy to the working muscles.

STRENGTH/RESISTANCE TRAINING

Resistance, strength and weight training are synonymous, and are used to describe exercise that requires the body's musculature to move against a force or resistance. The best example is weight training, but other forms of strength training can be done by using your own body weight, e.g. press-ups or sprint training.

FLEXIBILITY/STRETCHING/MOBILITY TRAINING

Flexibility and mobility are the ability to move through a full and normal range of motion. In the next section we will look deeper into the importance of the stretch.

TECHNIQUE

Everything should be done with perfect technique and remember: practice does not make perfect, practice makes permanent. Practice, badly done, becomes permanent; only perfect practice makes perfect. If you perform an exercise with poor technique you will increase the likelihood of injury and lose the benefit of the exercise. Improper technique occurs when we try to lift a weight that exceeds or is below our strength. When we rush or overtrain and are tired we are also vulnerable to injury.

Principles of Training

There are eight principles that must be understood and applied in training if success is to be achieved.

1. Specificity: Training effects are specific to the type of training undertaken. Don't swim every day if you want to run a marathon.
2. Reversibility: Training effects are reversible and will diminish if training is infrequent or too low in intensity. If you don't use it, you lose it!
3. Progressive overload: We must have overload in training if we want to achieve our goals; we do need to push ourselves so we feel we are using some effort. As we get fitter, we must progress our training to continue to benefit.
4. Recovery: Taking breaks can mean the difference between achieving your goals and ending up with an injury from overtraining.
5. Adaptability: When exercising, be adaptable to changes brought about by other influences: injury, pregnancy, shift work.
6. Variation: Keep training varied: gym work one day, walking another day, dancing, cycling on others. All help to alleviate boredom while keeping the body moving.
7. Individuality: Because the latest celebrity is achieving success with the latest exercise craze, does not necessarily mean you will get the same results. The programme needs to suit you as an individual.
8. Goal Setting: Realistic goals should be set, long and short-term, to act as a reward. Write them down and refer to them regularly.

AEROBIC TRAINING

Aerobic training should be seen as activities performed continuously for a minimum of 15–20 minutes at a high enough intensity to bring a warm colour to the face and an increase in heart rate and body temperature. This should be done no less than three times a week.

Aerobic training goes beyond merely attaining fitness: it defines the status of the heart muscle and the vessels it serves, while decreasing the risk of developing conditions such as heart disease and obesity. It helps us gain more stamina and endurance, resulting in less fatigue. It can make us more energetic at a small cost.

Benefits of Aerobic Exercise

1. Reduces blood pressure: High blood pressure is a major public health problem associated with increased risk of heart attack, kidney failure and stroke. The risk of developing these diseases more than doubles when blood pressure is greater than 140/90 and more than trebles when the blood pressure reaches 160/95. Studies show aerobic activity such as walking can reduce blood pressure significantly.
2. Decreases high cholesterol: It is now generally recognised that physical activity reduces high cholesterol, thus potentially reducing the risk of cardio-vascular disease.
3. Decreases body fat stores: Regular aerobic activity increases the body's ability to burn calories, thus reducing our body fat and reducing weight.
4. Increases work capacity: Physical activity will help us feel more energetic and improve our ability to complete daily tasks with less fatigue.
5. Increases wellness: Physical activity is associated with decreasing stress and anxiety. Aerobic activity is associated with releasing alpha waves in the brain; these waves are electrical brain patterns of activity that indicate the mind is relaxed. Physical activity stimulates the production of brain hormones called endorphins: these help block pain and create a euphoric state.
6. Increases the ability of the heart and lungs to function: Regular aerobic training increases the heart's ability to pump the blood and the lungs' ability to re-oxygenate the blood, resulting in less fatigue and stress.

MUSCULAR STRENGTH OR RESISTANCE TRAINING

This has received high acclaim in the last five years, especially with women who at one time shied away from it. It was thought that muscles formed by using weights and against resistance turned to fat or flab, and that strength training built big, bulging muscles. Now it is considered to be one of the best ways of reducing body fat and reshaping the body. Strength training appears not to increase blood pressure, but if it does increase, it is usually due to a diet too high in fat, or the use of steroids or over-training.

The bad news is that we lose approx 5–10 lbs of muscle every decade from the age of twenty, so the only way to stop this muscle loss is through strength training. If we concentrated only on aerobic training for weight loss, we would continually lose muscle and by the end of the year we would burn fewer calories and consequently gain body fat. This muscle loss also results in a reduction in the Basal Metabolic Rate (the body's ability to burn calories at rest). Strength training can increase the Basal Metabolic Rate by as much as 25% for up to 15 hours after training.

Benefits of Muscular Strength or Resistance Training:

1. Decreased body fat stores and increased metabolism. The more lean muscle we have, the more calories we burn at rest to maintain this muscle. It takes approx 76 kcal to maintain 1 lb of muscle.
2. Improved muscular strength and endurance.
3. Improved joint stability and ligament strength.
4. Improved nerve efficiency, coordination and motor skills.
5. Improved bone density and prevention of certain overuse injuries. Peak bone mass tends to be reached at about thirty years and tends to decrease after these years. Strength training increases bone density while providing muscular balance to help prevent injuries. The key word here is balance. Doing press-ups for the upper body must be balanced with back work to avoid injury.
6. Strengthened back and improved posture. Most of the population will experience moderate to severe back pain at some stage in their lives, so a preventative or recuperative measure is imperative. Sedentary lifestyle results in muscle loss, weight gain and muscular imbalances, often leading to pain and immobility. There are specific exercises which we will look at later to aid in back stability and strength.
7. Increase in GTT. One six month study found an increase in gastrointestinal transit time (GTT). This is the body's ability to go to the toilet. Strength training helps aid and prevent Irritable Bowel Syndrome, cancers and digestive disorders and diseases.
8. Improved Glucose uptake. Strength training has been reported to increase glucose uptake in the muscles by as much as 26%, which is important in dealing with obesity and diabetes.
9. Increased functional power and speed abilities on the sports field.

If we lose 5–10 lbs of muscle every decade, and our dietary intake is staying the same or even increasing, we are seriously heading for increased weight and body fat.

Muscle loss from inactivity = a lower energy output.

Dietary intake fuels energy output. If muscle loss is significant, the result is a huge drop in energy output. When dietary intake is not reduced:

Body fat goes up = Middle Age Spread.

However, it is avoidable.

STRETCHING/FLEXIBILITY/MOBILITY TRAINING

The importance of stretching tends to be overlooked and misused. What must be understood is that if we exercise, we must stretch: it is a critical factor in injury prevention and performance and an absolute essential component of wellness.

Flexibility is the ability to move through a full and normal range of motion. A number of factors can limit our ability to do this, in particular, genetic inheritance and our training programme (or lack of it). Poor technique can result in shortening our range of motion. Flexibility training helps balance muscle groups and minimise injury risk. Most importantly, flexible joints require less energy to work so flexibility training helps enhance our energy.

Several studies have indicated a distinct relationship between age and the degree of flexibility: we can expect to lose 40% of our mobility between the ages of forty and seventy. After the age of twenty-five, normal ageing tends to accelerate, causing significant change in connective tissue and eventually decreased extensibility in the muscle.

Why Stretch?

1. Helps reduce the natural tendency of the body to lose mobility.
2. Increases circulation and nutrient transport to a muscle.
3. Improves muscle group balance to aid posture.
4. Improves recovery time after activity. When a muscle is worked, even in a low intensity activity that may only take fifteen minutes, there is a small degree of local cell damage along with a lot of blood being pumped into the muscle. Some debris can remain in the muscle after exercise, leading to muscle soreness, stiffness and even injury. When a muscle is stretched, we get muscle lengthening after about fifteen seconds. Once the muscle lengthens, we get an increase in blood flow to that area, nutrients are carried straight to the site, debris is carried away and the repair process starts. This increases the benefits of the next training session.

WHEN TO STRETCH

If you are looking for real gains in mobility, stretching at the end of each session should be a significant part of your programme. People who stretch before runs could cause as much injury to themselves as the run itself. A warm-up should not include a stretch. If someone gets injured, it is most likely not because they missed the stretch prior to activity, but started the activity too quickly. Typical is the footballer who did not exercise off-season, and when the season starts, throws himself into the game without being fit enough. If he lasts the start of the season but fails to stretch after each game, he will be very lucky if he avoids injury.

TAKE CARE

Too much of anything can have negative effects. Instability caused by overstretching to ligaments can lead to degenerative joint change such as arthritis. Stretch for at least 10–15 minutes after each game or exercise routine. For real improvements in mobility, a comprehensive stretch routine should be undertaken as well as the training programme.

Warming up

means increasing heart rate and body temperature. If we stop and stretch we end up cooling the body back down and going into the activity cold. Rod Pope, a physiotherapist with the Australian military tested this out on 2500 recruits a year. He has come to the conclusion that it may cause more harm than good to stretch prior to activity.

Aerobic training results in

Reduction in blood pressure
Decreased bad cholesterol
Decreased body fat stores
Increased aerobic work capacity
Decreased clinical symptoms of depression, stress and anxiety
Increased heart and lung function

Strength training results in

Decreased body fat stores
Increased metabolism
Improved muscular strength and endurance
Improved joint stability and ligament strength
Improved bone density
Strengthened back, improved posture and decreased risk of injury
Increased glucose uptake by the muscles
Improved gastro-intestinal transit times

Stretching results in

Reduction in the natural tendency of the body to lose mobility
Increased circulation and nutrient transport to a site
Improved muscle group balance to aid posture
Improved recovery time post activity: decreased residual tension in a muscle.

When we look at the stretch we hear of many different styles and techniques. From static to ballistic, PNF (Proprioceptive Neuromuscular Facilitation) to MET (Muscle Energy Technique). PNF, MET and ballistic tend to be for the advanced training individual. We require a good level of both fitness and mobility to partake in these forms of stretching.

SAFETY ASPECTS OF EXERCISE

Warm Up

The typical walker or runner tends to start into training too fast and stressed. We should always start our activity slowly and gradually build the intensity; this helps to prevent injury.

Skeletal muscles should never be worked when cold, they should be warmed up. The warm up makes the muscle more pliable, in turn reducing the risk of injury. When we are active, the body, in particular the muscles, will be under stress, so we need to allow it to adapt to these stresses. We do that by starting slowly and gradually building up the intensity. What is important to understand, is that the warm up is preparation for training. It should not stress the body's systems, and instead improve the quality of training. Recommended guideline is ten to fifteen minutes. The fitter we are, the less time needed for a warm up, but a warm up must always be done.

Cool down

This tends to be overlooked, usually due to time limitations. If we do this, we are failing to properly plan out an exercise schedule. If warm up is important as preparation for training, cool down is equally as important ,as it is the first stage of recovery leading to more quality training on the next activity session.

When we exercise muscles, a lot of blood is pumped into the muscle. If we suddenly stop exercising, we are left with blood pooling in the worked muscles and waste products left in the muscle. This can lead to muscle soreness and injury.

Basic Training Terms

Repetition (Rep): One complete movement of an exercise. It normally consists of two phases: a shortening and then a lengthening of a muscle.

Set: A group of repetitions performed without stopping.

Cool down also allows nerve function to readjust. Physical activity requires a great number of messages to be sent around the body. We should gradually bring the body down from activity to allow nerve function to readjust. It also allows the heart rate and body temperature to return steadily to normal. The post stretch, described earlier in *When to Stretch* should be incorporated into all activity as part of the cool down.

Monitoring Exercise Intensity

RPE (Recommended Perceived Exertion) is the most recommended form of training for the non professional, while Target Heart Rate is used for the professional.

It is simple and functional, assigning a numerical value to how you feel during the exercise routine; it is sometimes called the *Borg Scale*. It takes into account how you feel in terms of exertion and muscular fatigue.

The scale is measured from 0 – 10 in relation to exertion: 0 for nothing at all, 10 for maximum work. Ideally we should be exercising somewhere between 4 and 6.

RPE

0: Nothing at all
1: Very Weak
2: Weak
3: Moderate
4: Somewhat strong
5: Strong
6: Strong
7: Very Strong
8: Very Strong
9: Very Very Strong
10: Maximum Effort

Intensity by the Korvonen Formula

This is a system for the fitter reader to work out his/her training heart rate. This involves heart rate monitoring using a chest strap and watch. We use the '220 minus age' formula for determining maximum heart rate.

Predicted maximum heart rate minus resting heart rate
Multiply the answer by desired intensity (50–80%) and add resting heart rate.
The answer will give us a perceived target heart rate.

For example a forty year old man for whom a desired intensity is 70% and resting heart rate is 80 beats per minute:
220 – 40 = 180 (predicted maximum heart rate)
180 – 80 = 100 multiplied by 70% = 70, + 80 = 150 target heart rate.

How we work it out:

Training heart rate = Maximum heart rate – Resting heart rate
Multiplied by desired intensity (50–85%)
+ Resting heart rate

Eg: What is the training heart rate for a 40 year old woman with a resting heart rate of 80 beats per min at a desired intensity of 70%?

220 – 40 = 180 (predicted max heart rate)
180 - 80 (Resting heart rate) = 100
Multiplied by 70 (70% intensity) = 70
+80 (resting heart rate) = 150, target heart rate at 70%

Remember, this is only perceived, as the predicted maximum heart rate was taken from 220 minus age, and not an actual functional capacity test.

EXERCISE FOR HEALTH

Walking for Health

Walking is one of the most common forms of aerobic conditioning activity and, with low injury rate, functional adaptability and simplicity, is useful for those with a sedentary lifestyle trying to become active.

If new to walking, stay on the flat as much as possible, avoid hills and inclines. Once you get into walking, three days a week for two weeks, you should be able to introduce a more hilly terrain, but use Recommended Perceived Exertion (RPE) scale and try to stay in the region of 5–6. When we tell people to walk at a faster pace, it is a fast pace for yourself and should not be measured against others.

As you get more used to the activity, try not to fall into a comfort zone of training. This can easily happen as the body adapts easily. The result is our gains tend to plateau off. Try the '5 off, 1 on' routine: walking at your normal pace for 5 minutes, and at an accelerated pace for 1 minute, then back to normal pace for 5 minutes. If you are quite fit and not overweight, to increase energy cost and get better value for your time, try a 1 minute jog between 5 minute walks.

Another simple way to avoid the comfort zone is to change the direction of your walk. Vary the places you walk, from road to sand to incline and hills.

Rather than focusing on distance, I like to see people focusing on time. Starting with 20 minutes, 40 minutes is a sufficient target for a walk. If you are very fit, you can go longer distances, but try to focus on the quality not quantity.

The latest aid to walking is the pedometer, which is used to measure the number of steps taken. In Japan, epidemiologists have recommended adults should walk at least 10,000 steps per day to maintain optimum health.

Jogging and Running for Health

Naturally enough, jogging and running put greater demands on the body's systems than walking, in turn creating higher energy expenditure. An addictive form of training, be careful to make sure you are fit enough to start. Try to avoid too many declines; downhill running can create some injury problems. If you are very fit and in good form on your run, you could introduce a little bit of sprint training to your routine.

Cycling for Health

Cycling is another great form of activity where you can get to enjoy the fresh air and scenic views. You can make it as difficult as you want, adding fast sprints and hilly routes, but start on the flat. Always wear a helmet and plenty of luminous clothing at night.

Bicycle seat height should be set high enough so that on the bottom of the down stroke, the leg is not quite completely extended, allowing a soft bend in the knee. This will help to avoid knee trouble later.

Gym Work for Health

For those using the gym, it is not enough to do 20 minutes on the stepper, 10 minutes on the bike, 10 minutes on the treadmill, 10 minutes on the cross trainer, a few stretches, and no weight training. Ensure the programme is designed for you and your goals. This means discussing your health history with a trainer and seeing how to fit an appropriate amount of training into the time you can spare in the gym.

For best results, combine both cardio-vascular training with strength and flexibility training. If you have only a 30 minute workout, the programme must be designed to get the maximum value for that time.

Swimming/Aqua Activities for Health

Swimming and aquatic activities are great as they reduce stresses and impact on the body. (The breast stroke is not the ideal stroke, as it can cause strain on the neck and lower spine. It's the easiest to do, but not the best for avoiding damage.) While sauna, steam room and jacuzzi are relaxing, we need to get into the pool to exercise. Using push and pull and double concentric movements, there should be no muscle soreness after activity. The great thing about the water is you are working against a resistance which strengthens the body without stressing it.

Don't forget to drink some water during swimming sessions. It is easy to forget when surrounded by it!

Group Training

This is a studio session, usually in a gym, where a group of people trains together under instruction. This can be great fun and sociable. The group energy can carry you on a low-energy day, and meeting friends is further motivation to keep going.

Yoga, Pilates, aerobics, circuit training and other forms of training classes are held in many community schools and are ideal for those not members of a gym.

Strength Exercises

These exercises can be introduced before or after any physical activity, once a warm up has been done. If you train in a gym, these exercises may not be necessary, as you may already be doing strength training as part of a programme. At home they can be added after a walk or cycle.

We aim for overload in training, and strength exercises can provide this muscular overload. This is not about pain, but you should be aware that you are working your muscles and are putting in effort.

Good technique is essential, quality always followed by quantity. Follow the step-by-step guide to doing these exercises and always recheck your technique. Use slow and controlled movements throughout. Faulty technique, even by only a slight error, can lead to the targeted muscle not doing the job and to injury.

1. Squat

This is a difficult exercise and requires a great degree of technique.

Muscle Groups Worked:	The prime movers are the legs and bum while the back plays a large role in stabilising.
Breathing	Breath in as you squat down, breath out on the way up
Body Alignment	Feet slightly wider than hip distance apart, very slight point out on toes. Legs straight, but knees not locked out. Standing tall, head in a neutral position, tummy tight. Without lifting the head make eye contact high on wall in front.
Beginner	Grip the back of a strong chair to allow balance.
Intermediate	Place hands on opposite shoulders, forearms crossed.
Advanced	Cup a two litre filled bottle of water into cupped arms
Technique	Keeping tummy tight, no pelvic tilt. Squat down allowing knees to travel forward. Keep lowering yourself down without allowing the heels to leave contact with the floor. Allow the thighs to go past parallel to the floor. Without bouncing push upward, using the legs and bum, to a standing position.
Common Mistakes	Travelling forward from the hip rather than knee. Rounding the back and collapsing the chest. Pushing up with the hip rather than the legs. Hip swaying to one side. Allowing heels to lift or using a support under the heels. Knees tracking in or out. Knees falling in or out.
Tips	If you are having a problem with balance fix your eyes onto a point high above you but keep the head neutral.

You may frown and gasp at the technique provided for the Squat. One thing I would say is: remember, it is an advanced movement. If you don't have the mobility to complete the exercise, improve your mobility and co-ordination with other exercises and try this one again later.

beginner

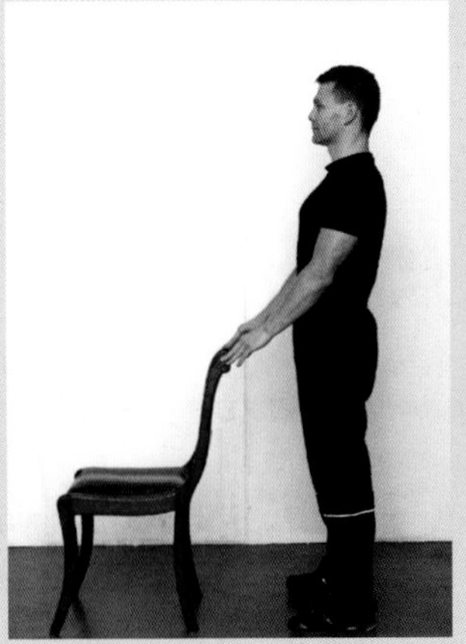

advanced

2. Leg Lunge

Muscle Groups Worked	The main prime movers are the legs and bum. The lower back plays a big role in stabilising.
Breathing	Breath in as you lower, breath out on return.
Body Alignment	Standing tall, feet hip distance apart. Head neutral, tummy tight. Take a large step forward, not too long, and keep the feet hip distance apart. Hold the position. The rear foot should be up on the ball of the foot.
Beginner	Place the hand on the same side as the leg you stepped forward with onto the hip. Support the forearm on the side of the rear leg onto the back support of a chair.
Intermediate	Both hands placed onto hips.
Advanced	Two 500ml bottles of filled water in each hand, held down by the side.
Technique	Bend the leading leg at the knee, while also bending the back knee. Keep the chest tall, lower the hips, bending in from the front knee. Push back to starting position and on completion of desired repetitions, change legs.
Common Mistakes	Banging the knee of the back leg off the floor. Dropping the body forward as you bend in on front knee.

beginner

intermediate

advanced

3. Lateral Step Up

Muscle Group Worked	The musculature of the leg and knee.
Breathing	Breath in as you lower, breath out on return.
Body alignment	Standing tall, head neutral, tummy tight.
Beginner	Both feet off the step prior to movement, allow both hands to be supported to aid balance.
Intermediate	One foot on step, other foot off step and suspended.
Advanced	(Peterson Step Up) Place foot on step, slightly pointing out, other foot on the floor. Ensure the back of the heel is in line with the front of the foot of the trailing leg. Now raise the heel of the trailing leg so you are high on the ball of the foot
Technique	Use the first step of a stairs or a large phonebook, 4–6 inches for all levels. Beginner will step well in and up on the step, placing feet together ensuring the knee of the stepping leg stays with the ankle. Complete desired repetitions and change sides. Intermediate will bend the standing knee allowing the suspended leg to lower but only slightly. Complete desired repetitions and change legs. Advanced, lift the leg off the floor by pressing in the ball of the foot and down through the knee and rolling back onto the heel of the foot on the step. Slowly roll back onto ball of the foot lowering the elevated leg back to starting position.
Common Mistakes	Knee falling in or out. Hips twisting rather than bending in from knee. Hips twisting as knee bends rather than travelling back.

beginner

intermediate

advanced

4. Leg Curl

Muscle Group Worked	The muscles of the back of the upper leg
Breathing	Breath in as you lower and out on lifting.
Body Alignment	Standing tall, head neutral, tummy tight. Legs straight but knees not locked out. Place stool at back of legs, lower leg distance. Try to ensure the stool is heavy and won't topple during movement. Use wall to maintain balance
Technique	Curl easily up on one leg till heel makes contact with the underneath of the seat of stool. Pause and push heel against stool for two seconds and gently release and lower. Do desired repetitions and change legs.
Common Mistakes	Too fast a movement. Leaning forward.

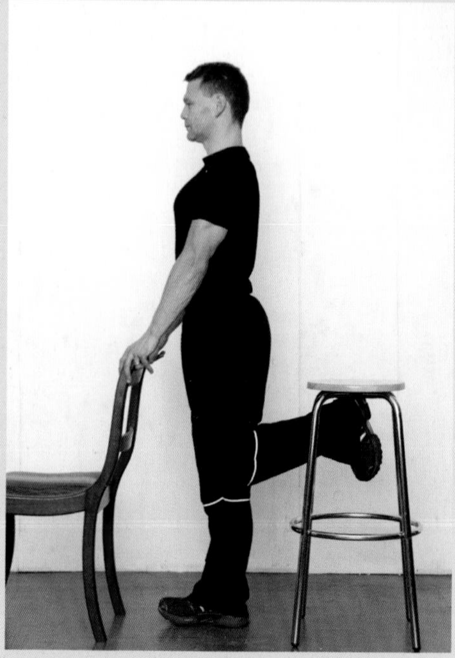

5. Standing Heel Raise

Muscle Group worked	The muscles of the lower leg.
Breathing	Breath in as you lower, breath out on return.
Body alignment	Standing tall, head neutral, tummy tight. Legs straight but knees not locked out. Balls of the feet onto a step or phone book, heels extending over edge. Use wall or chair for support/balance.
Technique	Lower heels to floor, then push up high onto balls of the feet, hold and contract calf muscles of lower leg. Repeat. If you can control balance, take hands off chair.
Common Mistakes	Pushing up onto the outside of the feet rather than the balls of the feet. Hips swaying forward on the push, or swaying back as you lower. Putting too much body weight onto support.

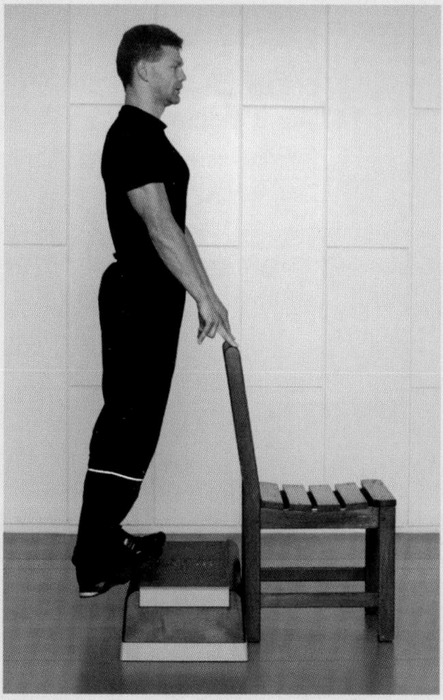

6. Press-Up

Muscle Group worked	The muscles of the chest, shoulders and arms.
Breathing	Breath in as you lower, breath out on return.
Beginner	On all fours, hands placed slightly beyond shoulder width. Tummy tight and head neutral. Try to ensure the bodyweight is forward, not back. Ensure the hands are supporting the body weight, not the hips or legs. You might need to walk the hands forward without letting the legs follow. Try to place padding under the knees.
Intermediate	Position as above but cross the ankles and lift the feet.
Advanced	Position as above but on the balls of the toes.
Technique	Lower the chest to the floor by allowing the arms to bend. There is a slight lean forward as you lower. To ensure the chest aligns itself with the hands, the shoulders should not align themselves with the hands. Just as the chest gets close to the floor push up to starting position and repeat movement.
Common mistakes	Not lowering close enough to the floor. Dropping hips, not the chest, to the floor. Allowing the hips to stay higher than the back. On lowering aligning the shoulders up with the hands. Locking out the elbows as you straighten.

If you find this exercise difficult, try a seated push up.

Sit on a chair, chest tall, hands at shoulder-width distance placed beside the bum. Push the hands into the chair, trying to lift bum and heels off the seat and floor and release back. This in time will help strengthen the upper body into doing a press-up.

beginner

intermediate

advanced

7. The Extension

Muscle Group Worked	The musculature of the back.
Breathing	Breath in as you raise, and breath out on lowering.
Body Alignment	Lying on tummy, elbows bent, forearms flat on ground. Hands slightly above shoulder height.
Technique	Lift up onto forearms, pushing chest up and out to roof. Pause at top of movement and slowly lower. Don't push with hands or arms, lift with back. No weight in the arms.
Common Mistakes	Pushing with hands and arms and not lifting with back. Initiating with the head rather than torso. Allowing the legs to move or lift. Pushing chest out to floor rather than up and out to roof. Extending and flexing the neck during the movement.

If you are strong and advanced, just at the top of the extension lift the forearms slightly off the floor, squeezing the shoulder blades. Pause and release slowly. Repeat. Six reps in any one set is enough of this exercise.

correct

incorrect

8. The Flying Superman

Muscle Group Worked	The musculature of the back and pelvic floor.
Breathing	Breath in on lifts, breath out as you lower.
Body Alignment	Lying on tummy, arms stretched out in front of body.

To do this exercise correctly, first learn how to activate the navel. What I mean by this is draw the belly button inwards. Standing, place two fingertips onto your navel. This is a small movement; don't make it a large one. It is not about sucking in the stomach. Draw the navel ever so slightly away from the fingertips. Don't allow movement come from above the navel, but from below it (as if you are trying to stop yourself from going to the toilet). Breathe normally without deactivating navel.

Technique	Activate navel. Imagine a euro coin under navel and lift navel slightly off coin, using the muscles below the navel. The navel must stay activated through each movement. Lift left arm, and gently lower, lift right arm and gently lower. Lift left leg and gently lower, lift right leg and gently lower. Alternate left leg and right arm at the same time and gently lower. Then lift right leg and left arm and gently lower.
Common Mistakes	Allowing navel to be deactivated on lifts of limbs. Trying to lift limbs too high. Allowing limbs to travel out rather than straight up and down.

9. Seated Pulls

Muscle Group Worked	The musculature of the back and arms.
Breathing	Breath in on pull, breath out on release.
Body Alignment	Sitting on seat, back not supported. Sitting tall, exaggerated lift on chest, head neutral.
Technique	
Beginner	Hands placed on knees. Depress and retract shoulders sliding hands back along the thighs. Push chest up and out and squeeze shoulder blades together. Pause and release back to starting position. Ensure head stays neutral.
Intermediate/Advanced	Bring arms out in front of body, slightly higher than shoulders. Depress and retract shoulder, leaning back from the hip. Pull arms back and down pushing chest up and out. Pause and release back to starting position.
Common Mistakes	Allowing the head to move forward and chin to jut out. Pulling with the arms rather than initiating with a retraction and depression in the shoulders. Allowing the chest to collapse. On pulling the arms down, allowing them to come in.

beginner

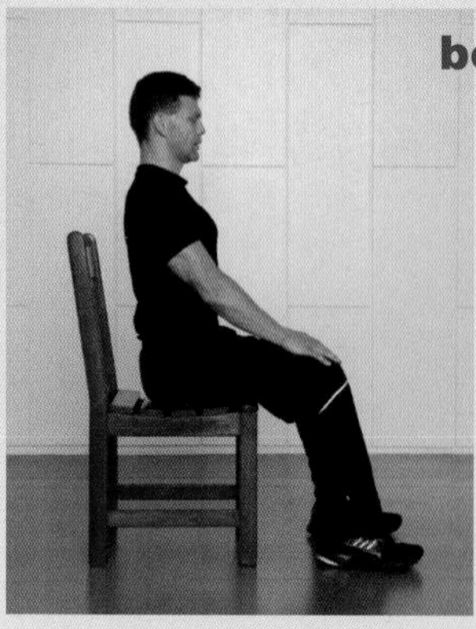

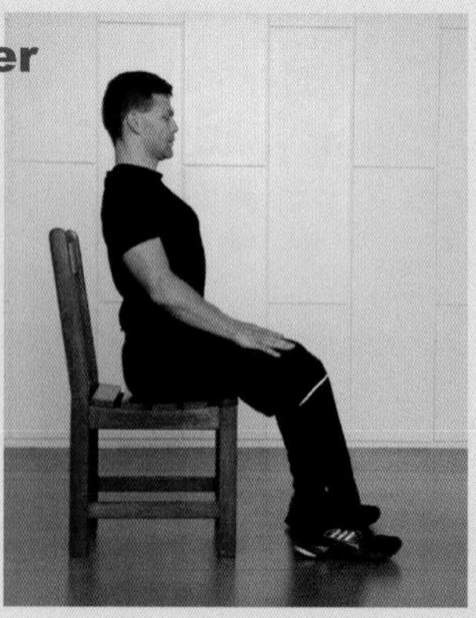

intermediate/advanced

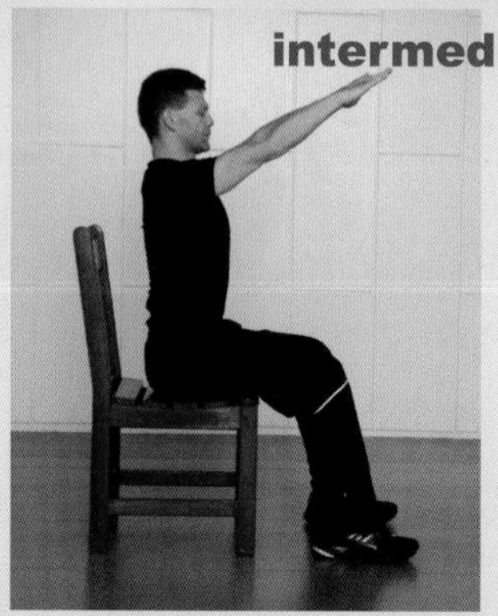

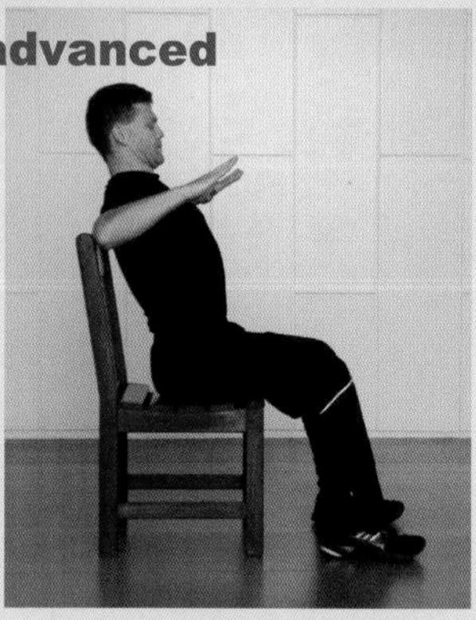

10. Pull Over

Muscle Group Worked	The muscles of the back, chest, ribs and arms.
Breathing	Breath in as you reach back, breath out as you pull.
Body Alignment	Lying on your back, knees bent, tummy tight, no pelvic tilt. Arms held straight up, soft bend in elbow, just over the chest. If intermediate or advanced you can hold a 2 litre bottle of water in each hand. If a beginner, just hold a rolled towel.
Technique	Lower the water/towel behind and away from you, creating the movement from the shoulder joint, not the elbows. Pull back to starting position.
Common Mistakes	Bending or straightening arms, must hold soft bend through the movement. Lifting the head or bum off the floor. Not having the knees bent.

correct

correct

incorrect

11. Lateral Raise

Muscle Group Worked	The muscles of the shoulders and arms.
Breathing	Breath in as you raise and out as you lower.
Body Alignment	Feet hip distance apart, standing tall, tummy tight, head neutral. Knees soft, when you soften your knees allow the bum to sit back so there is a slight lean forward from the hip, but keep chest tall. Hold a 500 ml bottle of water in each hand, in front of the thighs, allow bend in elbows.
Technique	Without any torso movement upward and out to side, lift with the elbow to shoulder height, pause and slowly lower.
Common Mistakes	Allowing the body to sway as you lift or lower. Jutting the chin forward as you lift. Allowing the chest to collapse as you lower.

12. Forward Raise

Muscle Group worked	Shoulders and arms.
Breathing	Breath in as you raise and out as you lower.
Body Alignment	Feet hip distance apart, standing tall, tummy tight, head neutral. Knees soft, when you soften your knees allow the bum to sit back so there is a slight lean forward from the hip, but keep chest tall. Hold a 500 ml bottle of water in each hand in front of thighs.
Technique	Without any torso movement, keeping the arms straight, lift each bottle in turn forward and out at arms length, pause and slowly lower.
Common Mistakes	Allowing the body to sway as you lift or lower Jutting the chin forward as you lift. Allowing the chest to collapse as you lower.

13. Bicep curl with half twist

Muscle Group Worked	The arms.
Breathing	Breath in as you raise, breath out as you lower.
Body Alignment	Feet hip distance apart, standing tall, tummy tight, head neutral. Knees soft, when you soften your knees allow the bum to sit back so there is a slight lean forward from the hip, but keep chest tall. Hold a 500 ml bottle of water in each hand by the side.
Technique	Curl the bottle of water upwards towards the shoulder, rotating the wrist. Curl the wrist until the bottle is facing the shoulder. Resist, and lower slowly back to starting position, and then do the other arm.
Common Mistakes	Not rotating the wrist fully. Not creating the movement from the elbow. Swinging the shoulder or swaying the body. Not straightening the arms fully.

14. Dips

Muscle group Worked	The arms.
Breathing	Breath in as you lower, breath out on push.
Body Alignment	Sit on strong supportive seat. Palms resting, shoulder-width distance on seat. Walk feet out so bum is off seat and body weight is in arms, keep the chest tall, and bum close to the seat. Ensure the arm is straight but not locked out.
Technique	Bending the arm gently lower the body straight down, and push back up to starting position. During the movement ensure bum stays close to seat and chest stays tall.
Common Mistakes	Arms barely bend and the movement is created by bringing the bum away from the seat. Shrugging the shoulders. Not straightening the arms.

correct

correct

incorrect

ABDOMINALS

Whenever I ask clients what their goals are, abdominal training is always one of the top priorities. Even though it is one of the most popular areas to be trained, it seems to be the least understood.

The abdominals are seldom required to lift the torso against gravity, yet most people train their abdominals exclusively that way. That is not to say that abdominal curls are wrong or bad, but when performed in isolation this exercise may not be enough to develop the desired musculature.

The front muscle wall, the rectus abdominis: This appears to be the muscle we all focus on. It attaches from the chest and lower ribs and inserts into the pubis. It is strengthened by a strut of connective tissue which runs the length of the muscle. It flexes the body; the amount of flexion is individual and depends on your mobility and abdominal strength.

There are also oblique muscles that need to be exercised. These are not frontal muscles; their fan-like fibres extend all the way around the sides of the trunk.

The deepest layer is the transverse abdominis.

Abdominal exercises alone will not flatten a stomach. Other exercise and a change in eating habits are also needed. You can't work the lower abs without working the upper abdominal region. It is one muscle, so work on both regions is necessary. We can work the obliques separately because the fibres of the muscle sweep differently.

The reason we probably feel the tummy curl more in the lower abdominal region is due to leverage. The lower body is the anchor and the upper body the lever.

70% of the front abdominal muscle is located above the belly button and 30% is located below.

15. Abdominal Exercises

Sit down, nice and tall, feet hip distance apart, and relax (not slouch). This takes some concentration. Take a deep breath in, and when you breathe out, try and contract the stomach. Don't blow the belly out or suck it in. Ensure the posture does not collapse when breathing out or in.

Try to imagine bringing the top and bottom of the stomach together. Another good way to practise is to imagine someone is slapping you in the stomach. There is a slight drawing in and then a tightening as you resist the slap.

Try doing five of these breaths, in and out. You will also feel a tightening around the back while you do this exercise.

Having mastered it five times, try doing it with a leg lifted slightly off the floor. Don't allow the body to collapse to one side or allow the leg to move. Try doing five repetitions with the same technique as above and then change legs.

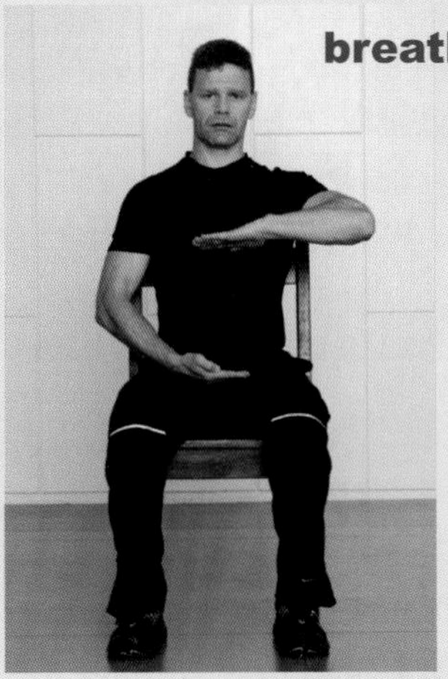

breathe in...

breathe out...

with leg lift

Try doing the contractions lying on your tummy, resting your chin on your hands.

Deep breath in, relax, breath out. Contract the tummy area with slight pulling and then a tightening.

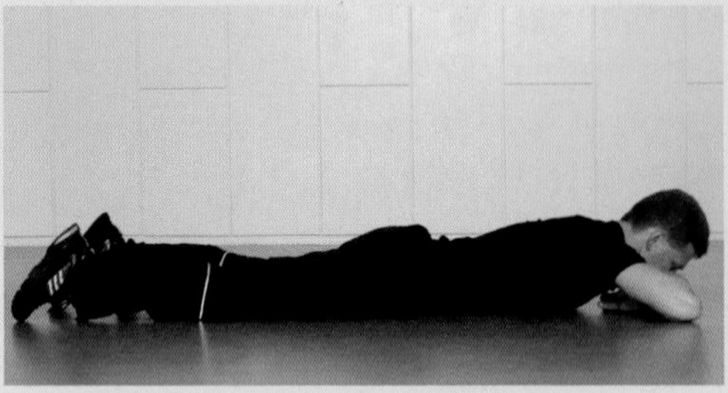

During abdominal curls, the head is a heavy part of the body. The neck can tire quickly and become sore and stiff. Try this technique for relief:

Clasp the fingers together. Bring your thumb pads together. The little fingers should not meet. Place the thumb pads at the base of your skull, just where the neck meets the back of your head. Try it lying down, rest the head into the thumb pads of you hands, and allow it to take the weight of your head. Never pull the head. When you initiate movement, create it from the abdominals, curling the shoulders and allowing the head and hands to follow, keeping the weight of the head in the hands.

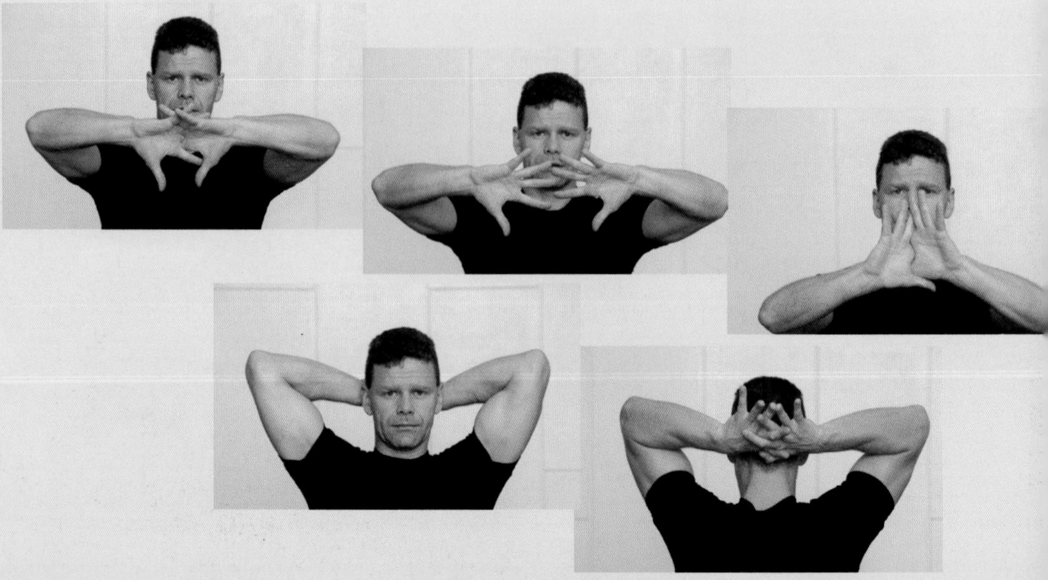

16. Abdominal Curl

Main Muscle Worked	Abdominals.
Breathing	Breath out as you curl up and inhale as you lower.
Body Alignment	Lying on your back, neck and shoulders relaxed. Put a soft bend in your knee so you are on your heels, feet pointing to ceiling. Keep the feet hip distance apart. Clasp the fingers and place at the back of the head.
Technique	Try to initiate by tightening the abdominals and, curling the shoulders, allowing the head to follow. Ensure you curl in towards the knees rather than up straight. Pause and squeeze the abdominals tightly at the top of the movement, breathing everything out. When you fully exhale, slowly relax the tightness in the abdominals and allow the shoulders to lower back to the floor, breathing in. Don't allow the head to lower completely and make contact with the floor.
Common Mistakes	The most common mistake made with any abdominal curl is to pick a spot on the ceiling and try to look at it while you curl. This causes you to curl up rather than in. Pulling the head and neck. Holding the breath. Not focusing on the breathing and contraction.

17. Progression of Abdominal Curl

Main Muscle Worked	Abdominals.
Breathing	Breath out as you curl up and inhale as you lower.
Body Alignment	Lying on your back, neck and shoulders relaxed. Put a soft bend in your knee so you are on your heels, feet pointing to roof. Keep the feet hip distance apart. Clasp the fingers and place at the back of the head. Straighten one leg, lift it off the floor, keeping it straight. Keep it low to the floor.
Technique	Start by tightening the abdominals and curling the shoulders allowing the head to follow. Ensure you curl in towards the knees rather than up straight. Pause and squeeze the abdominals tightly at the top of the movement, breathing everything out. When you fully exhale, slowly relax the tightness in the abdominals and lower the shoulders breathing in. Don't allow the head to lower completely and make contact with the floor. Ensure that when you curl, the leg that is held slightly off the floor makes no movement. Do your desired repetitions and then change legs.
Common Mistakes	Allowing the leg to move as you curl. Bending the knee of the elevated leg.

STRETCHING

Stretches Post Activity

Main Muscle Mobilised	Lower back.
Body Alignment	Lying on back, head resting on floor, both knees bent.
Technique	Lift both knees off the ground, place both hands onto the knees and gently pull into chest. Hold for 20 seconds.
Common Mistakes	Head lifting off floor. Holding the breath.

Main Muscle Mobilised	Lower back, shoulder.
Body Alignment	Lying on your left side. Left leg straight, bend right knee aligning knee and hip. Pin right knee with left hand.
Technique	Pin right knee with left hand and rotate torso in the opposite direction straightening out right arm. Allow the head to move into a comfortable position. Hold for desired time (20 seconds) and change sides.
Common Mistakes	Not straightening bottom leg. Trying to force the stretch.

Main Muscle Mobilised	Back of leg.
Body Alignment	Lying on back, head in contact with the floor. Right knee bent, straighten left leg and rest onto floor, foot pointing to the ceiling.
Technique	Raise the straight leg up keeping it straight and catch the lower leg. Hold for the desired time (50 seconds). Change legs.
Common Mistakes	Lifting the hip off the floor. Allowing the stretched leg to bend. Lifting the head and shoulder off the floor.

If you have difficulty catching the leg, hook a towel around the sole of the foot and grip the towel ends, pulling up with each hand.

Main Muscle Mobilised	Front of leg.
Body Alignment	Lying on tummy, chin resting on left hand.
Technique	Bend right leg and catch right foot with right hand. Hold for desired time (30 seconds) and change legs.
Common Mistakes	Pulling foot to outside of hip and past the bum.

If you have difficulty doing this stretch lying down, try it standing, using a chair as a support. If standing, ensure both knees line up during stretch.

Main Muscle Mobilised	Front of upper leg and hip.
Body Alignment	Fold towel into a cushioning square. Assume the lunge position, but placing knee onto towel. Hold a tall posture.
Technique	Step front leg forward pushing back leg back, opening out the back foot. Ensure the front knee does not go over the front ankle, and ensure the back leg has an angled sweep. Hold for desired time (20 seconds) and change legs.
Common Mistakes	Front knee travelling too far forward. Back leg not sweeping back. Dropping the body forward.

back of leg

front of leg

front of upper leg and hip

Main Muscle Mobilised	The Lower leg
Body Alignment	Standing tall, feet hip distance apart. Both feet facing forward. Tummy tight.
Technique	Step in on one leg, bending in on the front knee. Place both forearms on the wall. Keep back leg straight and both heels in contact with the floor. Hold for desired time (50 seconds) and change legs.
Common Mistakes	Leaning in on hands instead of forearms. Feet pointing away. Heels lifting off floor. Allowing the hip to sag.

Main Muscle Mobilised	The shoulder and back of arm.
Body Alignment	Standing tall, knees soft bum back slightly. Tummy tight.
Technique	Bring right arm straight across chest, ensure no bend in elbow. Reach over the arm with the left hand catching above the wrist and pull across the chest. Hold for desired time (20 seconds) and change sides.
Common Mistakes	Bending the elbow. Allowing the stretched arm's shoulder to rise up to ear.

Main Muscle Mobilised	Shoulder and neck.
Body Alignment	Standing tall, knees soft bum back slightly. Tummy tight
Technique	Bring arm up behind back and gently drop ear to opposite shoulder for 20 seconds.
Common Mistakes	Forcing a stretch.

lower leg

shoulder and back of arm

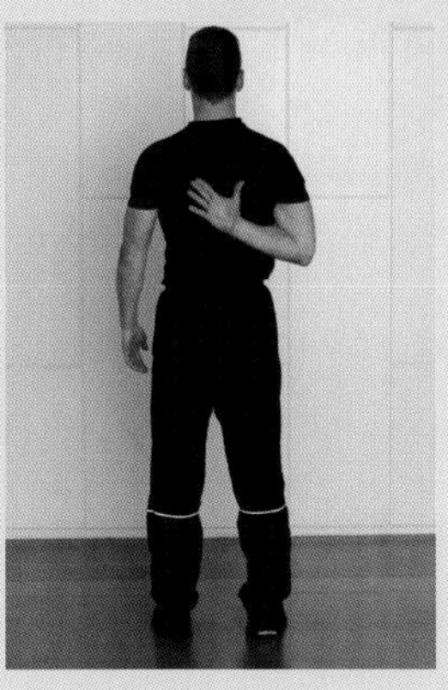

shoulder and neck

Seated Stretch

Main Muscles Stretched	Lower back and bum
Body Alignment	Sitting tall in chair, back not supported. Feet hip distance apart, Hand resting on legs.
Technique	Lift one knee off the floor and pull towards chest.
Common Mistakes	Leaning to one side. Pulling body to knee rather than knee to body.

Main Muscle Stretched	Lower back
Body Alignment	Sitting tall in chair, back supported. Feet hip distance apart.
Technique	Reach left hand around gripping top of chair and twist torso around, hold for desired length and change sides.
Common Mistakes	Torso collapsing.

Main Muscle Stretched	Back of leg.
Body Alignment	Sitting tall in chair, back supported. Feet hip distance apart. Phone book in front of foot of leg to be stretched.
Technique	Place heel onto phone-book, toes pulled back. Lean in from hips pushing chest out towards knee. Keep knee straight. Hold for desired time and change legs.
Common Mistake	Rounding the back and collapsing posture.

Main Muscle Stretched	Front of leg.
Body Alignment	Standing tall in front of stool. Feet hip distance apart. Ensure there is a wall adjacent for balance support
Technique	Place foot onto stool. Bend standing knee softly and sit bum back and down. Hold for desire time and change legs.
Common Mistakes	Placing shin onto stool.

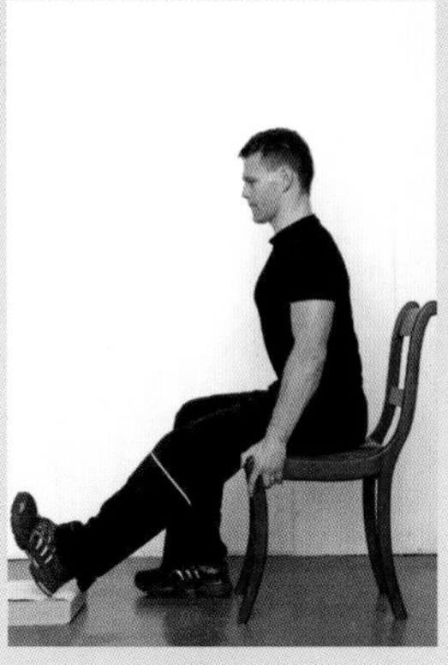

The good news is we don't always need to take ourselves down onto the floor to stretch. Whatever your reason for not being able to do stretches on the floor – lack of mobility, injury – try doing these stretches while seated and, if possible, later progress to the floor.

Here are combinations of exercise from which to choose a programme.

Do the abdominals and post stretches after your physical activity.

Pick one leg exercise consisting of 2 sets of 12/8 reps, one chest exercise consisting of two sets 12/6 reps, 2 back exercises consisting of two sets of 12/8 reps. One shoulder exercise consisting of one set of 12/8 reps and every second Programme do the arm exercises consisting of one set of 12/8 reps Post activity. Take 30 seconds rest between sets, and 40 seconds between exercises.

Beginner change the programme every 10 weeks; intermediate every eight weeks; advanced every six weeks. This exercise selection is for the non-gym user, to introduce a good foundation of strength with home exercises. Even though we are classing some of the exercises as advanced, they are truly not advanced until sufficient weight is lifted to cause muscular fatigue within the desired repetitions. This can only be achieved in a gym setting.

Examples

30 minutes walk

Start with a 10 minute warmup of a very gentle walk, building up to a normal pace. Try 5 minutes normal pace, followed by 1 min fast pace.
Slow the walk down for the last 5 minutes

Exercise	Sets	Reps
Squat	2	8
Press-up	2	6
Seated Pulls	2	6
Extensions	2	6
Lateral Raise	1	8

Finish with the abdominals
Curl with both feet in contact with floor 1/15 reps.
Curl with one heel and change 1/8 reps each leg.
Finish with all post stretches shown.

10 weeks later

30 minutes walk starting with 10 minutes warm up of a very gentle walk and then built up to the normal pace. 5 minutes normal pace followed by 1 min fast pace. Slow the walk down for the last 5 minutes.

Exercise	Sets	Reps
Lateral Step up	2	8
Seated Press up	2	6
Flying Superman	2	6
Extension	2	6
Forward Raise	1	8
Arm Curl	1	8
Dips	1	8

Finish with the abdominals.
Curl with both feet in contact with floor 1/15 reps.
Curl with one heel and change 1/8 reps each leg.
Finish with all post stretches shown.

This is another style of training

30 mins walk

Exercise	Sets	Reps
Squat	2	8
Leg Curl	2	8
Press-up	2	8
Seated Pull	2	8

Break the routine down.
Do a set of squats, and take a break for 30 secs, do a set of curls, break for 30 secs and repeat. That is the squat and leg curl complete. Then do a set of press ups , take a break for 30 secs, do a set of seated pulls, break and repeat. Routine complete: finish with abs and stretch.

A more advanced style of programme is to split the days of training so that a three day routine involves most muscle groups. We have numbered them so that you can get into the habit of varying the combinations to make it interesting and beneficial. Focus on the muscle groups noted each day, so that they get a rest on the other days. For example, focus on shoulders and arm, on Day 1; Day 2, legs; and Day 3, chest and back. Finish each day with abs and stretch. With these split days I would advise you to bring your cardio training down from a 30 to a 20 min walk.

Buy Dumbbells for the advanced stage of exercises, but limit reps to 6 per set for the advanced squat.

Day 1: Shoulders and Arms

Exercise	Sets	Reps	Rest
A1 Lateral Raise	3	10	10 secs
B1 Dips	3	10	10 secs
B2 Arm Curl	3	10	1 min

Day 2: Legs

Exercise	Sets	Reps	Rest
A1 Squat	4	10	10 secs
A2 Leg Curl	4	10	1 min 30 secs
B1 Heel raise	2	12	1 min

Day 3: Chest and Back

Exercise	Sets	Reps	Rest
A1 Press Up	3	10	10 secs
A2 Seated Pull	3	10	30 secs
B1 Flying Superman	2	exercise	10 secs

How we apply this programme

Day 1: A1, 1 set of lateral raise to be completed 3 times with a 10 sec break between sets. Then we do a set of dips 10 sec break, arm curl, 1 min break. And repeat B1 and B2 twice more.

Day 2: Do 1 set of squats, 10 sec break a set of leg curls, 1 min 30 secs break. And repeat A1 and A2 3 more times. Once you have completed A1 and A2 in this fashion complete 2 sets of heel raise with 1 min between sets.

Day 3: Do 1 set of press ups, 10 secs break, 1 set of seated pulls 30 secs break and repeat twice more. Once you have completed A1 and A2 in this fashion do 2 sets of the flying superman with a 10 secs break between sets. Finish with ABS and stretch.

Technique: Keep movements controlled and smooth. When you want to overcome a resistance, accelerate; when you want to control a movement, decelerate. For example, in the press up, slowly lower the body to the floor and quickly push up. With the squat, keep it slow when lowering the bum to the floor, and accelerate when pushing up.

Healthy Eating and Sport: *safe*food guidelines

The principles of a healthy diet apply to both athletes and non-athletes: base your diet on starchy carbohydrates, eat at least five portions of fruit and vegetables a day, include some dairy or dairy alternatives, include small amounts of protein-containing foods and include very small amounts of foods and drinks high in fat and sugar. What differs is the quantities and proportions of these foods.

Carbohydrates: these are one aspect of the diet that an athlete should pay particular attention to. Carbohydrates are stored in the body as a substance called *glycogen* which is then used as an energy source for muscles. If an athlete does not eat enough carbohydrate rich foods than they will feel tired and their performance will be affected. The amount of carbohydrate-rich foods that an athlete requires depends on the frequency, duration and intensity of exercise. As a guide, base every meal on carbohydrate-rich foods such as breakfast cereals (preferably wholegrain or porridge-based), breads (preferably wholegrain), potatoes and rice, and consume a high carbohydrate snack between meals, e.g. fruit, low-fat yoghurt, wholemeal scone or fruit smoothie.

Protein: protein requirements for most athletes – except for those involved in endurance and strength sports – and non-athletes do not differ. Even for those athletes with higher protein needs a varied balanced diet will meet those increased requirements in most cases.

Fat: small amounts of fats should be included in all of our diets. High fat diets lead to weight gain and lower carbohydrate intakes.

Fluids: it is important to drink enough of fluids before, during and after exercise to prevent dehydration.

Eating around exercise: to ensure that glycogen stores are topped up as a general rule eat a high carbohydrate meal 2 to 4 hours before exercising and a carbohydrate-rich snack within two hours after an exercise session.

For more information on nutrition for sports please contact the *Irish and Nutrition Dietetic Institute* or ***safe*food**.

Over to you...

What you may have noticed missing from this book are exercises which use a ball: an activity which is predominantly seen in the fitness and rehab field at present. I have left these out of this book purposely, as the reason of this book is to introduce people to physical activity and try to give you a true understanding of exercise. I feel that most people have neither the strength nor co-ordination to partake in a lot of the exercises designed for the ball. I also feel that these exercises are given too freely and with a lack of understanding. I have no time for this type of training and see very little sense in performing such exercises. In my experience, I have seen these exercises lead to a loss of strength and functionality.

The last thing I have to say on this subject is Core Stability: all exercise done with correct form and technique requires the body to rely on core stability. Ball training is not the only way to develop good core stability. please remember this.

Remember that if you really want to achieve the goal of overload in your training you will need to apply more resistance as you get fitter and stonger. This exercise prescription is for developing a very good foundation of fitness and strength, and once the foundation is laid you must build upon it. This is done through a heavier resistance lifted as you get stronger.

Some of the new information I have given in this book may suggest that exercise theory is in a state of change, but whatever about finer details, the theory remains the same, and studies have shown it's efficacy. It is still always wise to insist exercises makes sense and to ask professionals about the theories behind them.

In this book you are enjoying the benefits of experience which have mapped out a road to a healthier life. The key is to clearly define your goals and plan your daily routines. While it has taken years to shape the body to how it is now, if you want to change it, it will take time and consequently some patience too. Try to get rid of the excuses and think about doing some aerobic conditioning, some strength training and some stretches. These will serve to condition your body, but they are also good for the mind, helping to free it from stress. Use this book to enhance your lifestyle and enjoy feeling and looking better.

I became a holistic therapist from personal experience of health problems and a sense that 'there must be more to life than this'. Everything I teach and talk about is something I have tried out myself and found benefits from. Of course I always ask for advice, read up and research material, but most importantly for me, I listen to my heart. It's never wrong, though I used to try and persuade it otherwise.

The terms 'holistic' or 'complementary' therapy may be relatively new, but the therapies have been around for centuries in many forms of healing and medical work. We know from ancient Indian, Greek and Chinese texts that the human body has been treated for prevention, maintenance and ill-health from a mind, body and spirit perspective. We also know from indigenous people the world over who are still using holistic therapies, that if we treat a problem, we have a cure, but if we get to its source and gain understanding, we then have healing.

Karen

If I treat someone with a tense neck and shoulders every week with massage therapy, they will get relief for a few days. However, if I can give them an appreciation that their hectic schedule, carrying too many family responsibilities and not getting any time to themselves is exacerbating the problem, then they can take the power of their health back into their own hands. It gives me huge job satisfaction to empower people to look after themselves physically, mentally, emotionally and spiritually.

It is very exciting that our national television channel has a health programme with a holistic therapist, a nutritionist and a fitness instructor and brings in the relevant medical experts when required. The emphasis is towards taking responsibility for our own health, and prevention is the key strategy. Our health system is currently overloaded. If we all took better care of ourselves, there would be a natural balance between the use of our excellent medical and holistic practitioners. It is heart-warming to see the number of medical centres opening with a mix of both.

The best way to find out about a holistic therapy is word of mouth, the local health food shop notice board, the Golden Pages (always look for qualifications and association membership) or a referral from your doctor. I recommend going for one treatment to see if you like it and if the therapist is the right one to help you. It may take a few sessions until you feel relief, but you should feel at least relaxed and calmer after the first one. Listen to your intuition.

YOGA

The word 'Yoga' means 'union' in the ancient Eastern language of Sanskrit; 'union' between your body, mind and spirit. It is a complete science of life that originated in India many thousands of years ago. It is the oldest system of personal development in the world. It includes gentle postures (asanas), special deep breathing (pranayama), relaxation and meditation techniques (yoga nidra) which improve your ability to deal with life's stresses and strains. It is simple to do, and one class a week for six to eight weeks is a good way to start to see if you like it. You will soon feel its amazing benefits: an improvement in your posture, muscle tone and sleep patterns, plus an ability to cope with stress, to name but a few.

People come to yoga class for many different reasons, such as keeping their body fit and supple or seeking help for a specific complaint like neck or shoulder tension. Some come because of a lack of energy or general ennui. To the beginner, yoga may seem like just a series of odd physical exercises with strange deep breathing. After practising for a matter of weeks, you will begin to realise why the yogis of India devised this excellent lifestyle system. If your body is relieved of tension from doing the asanas and your energies are uplifted from the yoga breathing, THEN the mind can ease and the body, mind and spirit will be in balance and harmony. Once this occurs you are free to live life to its fullest, flowing through life's ups and downs with impunity. No wonder many stars, musicians, sports people and celebrities practise regularly.

There are three main types in Ireland: Hatha, Iyengar and Ashtanga.

The difference in the pace of the types of yoga can be compared to different ball games. Hatha, the most popular type, is a bit like playing tennis. Iyengar, which focuses on detailed alignment, is like badminton. Ashtanga is a bit like playing squash. Just because you love tennis doesn't mean that one day you aspire to play squash. No one type is better than another. Yoga is not competitive and people move at their own pace. It's all about listening to your body and working from there.

HATHA YOGA

'Ha' means sun and 'tha' means moon', reminding us of the balance in life between opposites (yin and yang). This is the most popular and classic form of yoga on which most other types are based. Classes include stretching, breathing and asana practice, with a relaxation session at the end. It is done at a relaxed pace so it is an excellent way to combat stress. It was brought to the modern world by Sri Krisnamacharya who translated many ancient texts detailing yoga practices at the turn of the last century. This is suitable for beginners.

IYENGAR YOGA

This type is based on the teachings of BKS Iyengar. He was a student of Krisnamacharya, who took Hatha Yoga and developed it with a strong focus on precise postural alignment. It is ideal for people who are a bit more flexible and like the emphasis on highly detailed instructions.

ASHTANGA YOGA

This is a strong physical type of yoga developed by Pattabhi Jois, who was also a student of Krisnamacharya. It consists of a series of asanas, which form a sequence that takes one and a half to two hours to do. It is fairly rigorous and only the most hardy students or teachers themselves progress past the primary series. Ashtanga is great for those who are sporty and very flexible. Dress to sweat!

YOGA THERAPY

This type of Hatha Yoga was developed by Krisnamacharya's son, T. Desikachar, who worked with people, one-on-one, to help with specific ailments. So rather than attending a public class, you go to a yoga therapist who will do a detailed consultation first, then tailor-make an asana practice for you.

HOT YOGA

This type of yoga was developed in the US by Indian Bikram Choudry and was introduced to Ireland as Hatha Yoga in almost sauna-like conditions designed to detox the body.

DYNAMIC/VINYASA FLOW YOGA

This is also new to Ireland and is Hatha Yoga with the 'flowing' elements of Ashtanga Yoga.

Some people start with Hatha Yoga and then may move up to either Iyengar or Ashtanga. Some flexible people start with beginners Iyengar or Ashtanga Yoga. Many are very happy to stay with Hatha because of its relaxation and stress management benefits. To find a local class, go along to your nearest health food shop as most teachers advertise there. The Golden Pages and the internet are also good sources. Classes are usually one hour to an hour and a half, once a week for six/eight weeks and cost approx €85–€100. Traditionally yoga in Ireland was taught in school or community halls, but now we are catching up with the rest of Europe and the US with lots of bright, airy, purpose-designed yoga studios.

YOGILATES

This is an amalgam of yoga and pilates which is fairly new to Ireland. It was a natural progression to join both, as Joseph Pilates took much of the inspiration for pilates from ancient yoga techniques.

BODY SCULPTING

These classes teach you how to sculpt each part of your body in a fun and easy way. Everyone uses light hand weights and the pace is relaxed. The music has a good beat, but is not loud and pulsating, so it suits those who like to keep in shape but don't like the classic gym music loudness. Some classes specify that weights are provided, others ask you to bring your own.

PILATES

If you want to tone your abdomen and improve posture, this is definitely for you. If you can imagine the relaxed pace of yoga using simple floor exercises then you have an idea of what it offers. All the exercises focus on the 'core' of the body – the abdomen and the lower back. It is amazing how much strength you can gain in this area over a short amount of time. Some classes use props for certain exercises.

Our natural energy should flow freely throughout every system in the body, reaching all our cells. In theory, we should wake up every morning full of the joys of spring. In reality, many of us crawl out of bed exhausted. If you can imagine our energy like electricity, you know it's there but you can't see it. You know that a light switch has electricity stored behind it and you have to flick it on to activate the light to shine. In the same way our energy is stored in seven distinct places in the body called 'chakras' and we can activate the energy there by doing yoga. The word chakra means 'wheel' in Sanskrit, the ancient Indian language, as your energy whirrs around in a clockwise direction. Each chakra is located up the spine and skull and is close to an organ in our endocrine or hormonal system.

The Base Chakra is located at the pelvic floor and is associated with the reproductive organs.

The Sacral Chakra is just below the navel and is associated with the reproductive organs and adrenal glands.

The Solar Plexus Chakra is above the navel and below the centre of the ribs and relates to the pancreas which maintains our blood sugar levels.

The Heart Chakra is at the centre of the chest and relates to the thymus gland which is an important part of our immune system.

The Throat Chakra relates to the thyroid gland which governs our metabolism.

The 'Third Eye' Chakra between the eyebrows and above the nose is so called because at night when we dream with our eyes closed we 'see' images through this part of the body which links to our subconscious and our memory.

Finally the Crown Chakra is located at what was our fontanel (visible in new babies before it closes up) and relates to our pineal gland.

If through stress our energy system is flagging, we can boost it by doing yoga which gently stimulates the chakras to spin clockwise and in tempo with each other.

REFLEXOLOGY

Reflexology is a complementary therapy that activates the healing powers of the body. We know the ancient Egyptians and Chinese practised it, as they left many examples of its virtues in their copious writings and pictorial representations. The premise is that precise areas of the feet relate to particular parts of the body so the whole body can be treated via points called 'reflexes'. These reflex areas in the feet correspond to the nerve endings and energy meridians of the body (refer to section on chakras). Therefore, a sore shoulder's reflex area at the side of the foot, when massaged gently, feels slightly 'crunchy' and may be quite tender. This is the result of a build-up of salt crystals which may cause blockages along that nerve area. The reflexologist will work carefully to release the tension and restore the free-flow of energy to the area.

Firm, but gentle pressure, is applied using the therapist's thumb. The person having the treatment can feel different sensations and these are interpreted by the therapist to indicate which parts of the body may be out of balance. The therapist can tell much by the shape, colour and even the odour of the feet! Some reflexologists use talcum powder, while others use aromatherapy oils, depending on their personal preferences.

Reflexology, while stimulating the body's own healing mechanism, will relax you. It is effective with Irritable Bowel Syndrome, back pain, asthma, sinus problems, stress and many more conditions. It is particularly good for working on parts of the body that might be sore to touch due to injury, or for those who want a simple non-intrusive therapy. During the session your clothes are kept on as the reflexologist works on your feet while you can enjoy time to relax.

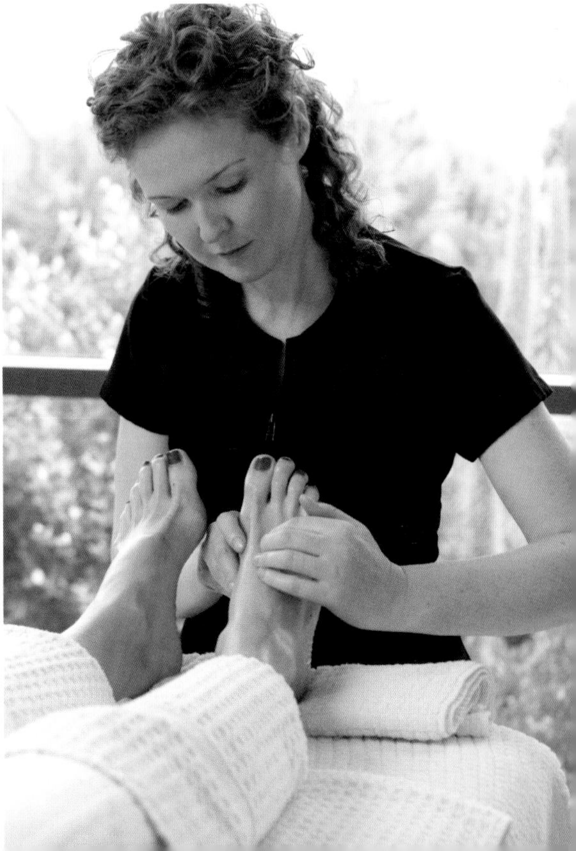

The reflexologist does not diagnose.

HOW CAN IT BENEFIT YOU?

By gently, but firmly, kneading a particular area, the reflexologist can ease away any build-up of tension or salt crystals in the area. Reflex areas are manipulated and massaged by the reflexologist to ease specific conditions, for example:

1. The big toe (the head area) for headaches and migraines.
2. The side of the foot (the shoulder area) for tense shoulders.
3. The centre of the foot (the relaxation point of the body) for stress.
4. The ball of the foot (the lungs) for asthma, colds, coughs, etc.
5. The small toes (the sinus points) for bunged up noses and sinuses.

This is a very relaxing therapy if you enjoy having your feet touched. The sessions usually take one hour to an hour and a half and cost €45–€60. The number of treatments needed depends on the problem. It is also a great preventative therapy.

MASSAGE THERAPY

We cannot underestimate the sense of touch: the nurturing hands of a mother, the caress of a lover, the soothing help of a nurse. Massage is one of the most ancient forms of therapy and uses certain key touch techniques designed to relax body and mind, ease any muscle knots or tension while boosting the body's energy levels naturally. An example is the effleurage massage stroke, which is a series of long sweeping movements that cover the back, leg or arm to stimulate the blood and lymph systems to warm the skin. At the same time the nervous system eases, and the energy system is enhanced, as the hands move along the meridians of the body.

At the consultation the therapist will take details, including previous injuries/medical conditions and any medication taken, and explain how the session will proceed. You will be asked to change into a warm towel and lie down on the massage plinth (like a doctor's table).

The massage therapist works in silence while you unwind listening to soothing music. Many people are surprised at the non-speaking element, unlike chatting at the hairdressers. It is more beneficial if the mind is allowed to relax fully by not talking, having pleasant thoughts such as visualising a favourite holiday scene.

A full body massage takes approximately one hour. A back, neck and shoulder massage lasts half an hour. Prices vary from city to country but generally an hour is €55–€60 and a half an hour is €30–€35.

INDIAN HEAD MASSAGE

Every day in India, in many family situations or even social gatherings amongst friends, Indian Head Massage is given between mother and child, father and son, husband and wife. It is a natural way of relieving stress and tension from the neck and shoulder area. Twenty years ago, Indian physiotherapist Nareda Mehta introduced Indian Head Massage at a London *Mind, Body, Spirit* exhibition. He combined the massage he received at home in India with techniques he learned as a physiotherapist and it was an instant success. This wonderfully relaxing treatment quickly spread throughout Europe.

Many of us carry tension in our heads which manifests as neck and shoulder pain, headaches, migraine, sinus problems, etc. This therapy is a gentle way to ease it while relaxing and soothing the body. Also, because no oil is used, it can be done through clothing and practised anywhere. It works well in a home or office environment.

The person being massaged sits in a chair, eyes closed. With a small cushion at chest level supporting the head, the therapist stands behind. The initial massage focuses on the neck and shoulders, moving to the head and finally to the face. Indian Head Massage also has a version using aromatherapy oils where you either sit or lie on a massage table, wrapped in towels.

Indian Head Massage takes half an hour and generally costs €30–€35.

BABY MASSAGE

Baby Massage is a wonderful way for the mother, father, grandparents, or other carers, to gently relax and calm a baby. It has been practised for thousands of years, ever since mothers realised that a relaxed baby is a happy baby.

The massage therapist teaches the mother/father how to massage their baby by demonstrating each simple move. Only one/two sessions with a qualified massage therapist are required to teach the techniques which can be done on the baby at home.

It is a lovely way to enhance the bonding between mother and baby and often between father and baby, especially if the baby is being breast-fed and the father has little close contact at feeding time.

The baby will respond to the feeling of light yet firm massage strokes by becoming calm and relaxed. Also, every time the baby is massaged, it knows that it is time to quieten down and play or sleep, depending on the time of the massage. A good time is after bath time so the oil moisturises the skin, or before bedtime, so the baby sleeps well. Sweet almond oil is used, as it is edible; most babies love to put things into their mouths including oily hands and feet!

The baby is put lying down with a favourite toy/rattle/soother.

Legs. Treatment always starts with the legs so the baby gets used to the feel of the oil. Nearly all babies love to kick and move their legs so the person massaging goes with this movement. The massage strokes are always firmly up towards the heart and lightly downward to the start position to aid circulation.

Abdomen. Here the massage strokes are in a clockwise direction, which is the direction of the digestion system. This greatly helps with any digestive problems.

Neck, Shoulders and Back. The baby sits up for this part. They usually prefer to sit than to lie on their tummies as they like to see what is happening.

Head. The baby sits up and the sweet almond oil is rubbed on the head – soothing and great for cradle cap.

In a massage clinic the first session is usually one hour and costs around €55. An outcall (where the therapist comes to your house) costs more: €60–€70, depending on distance. Further sessions can be set up if more tuition is required.

Most baby massage therapists advertise in local health food shops and the Golden Pages.

COUNSELLING AND PSYCHOTHERAPY

Mention counselling to most Irish people and they immediately think of the classic Woody Allen image of someone in a movie, lying on a couch with the 'shrink' asking strange questions twice a week for the rest of their lives. In reality, many Irish people attend Ireland's huge number of excellent counsellors and psychotherapists. We don't talk about it openly in case others think we're 'funny in the head'. One hundred years ago, every town and village had either a 'wise woman' or a 'good listener' who could be consulted in a discreet way to give impartial advice or be a friendly ear for the problem in hand. Many people find talking in confidence to their priest, pastor or rabbi has the same effect. In the busy world we live in, we frequently come across situations where we are stuck in a rut. The situation may be too personal to mention to a family member or friend. In fact, often it involves them, so it can be very isolating to try to figure it out alone. If there is no 'good listener' around to talk to, a counsellor can really help.

All of us have life problems from time to time, and sometimes we don't know how to get back on track. It helps to talk in confidence to someone who is trained to listen objectively and, most importantly, non judgementally, who can point us in the right direction towards ways to help ourselves.

HOW IT WORKS

There is a short consultation where details are taken and then the counsellor starts by explaining how the session/s will go. Generally they will ask you to start by talking about the problem in hand. Sometimes, especially the first time, you may not know where to start but anywhere that feels comfortable is good. They will ask you key questions as they listen to what you are saying in an objective way. Through talking and 'getting the problem off their chest', many people find that they get a perspective on the situation and that ways to deal with it emerge naturally. Imagine talking to an expert listener who has excellent insight into your problem and you'll have a fairly good idea how it works.

Psychotherapy is a more indepth way of working with clients who have more complex issues. It links past history with present problems and allows clients to have a better understanding of themselves while feeling able to cope with negative emotions. The psychotherapist is trained to use techniques that help to gain insight into unconscious behavioural patterns.

SITUATIONS IT CAN HELP

Stress is a fairly classic reason to seek help from a counsellor/ psychotherapist. Also depression, bereavement, unresolved anger and relationship difficulties. Then there are particular conditions such as obsessive-compulsive disorder, insomnia, constant worrying and eating problems. If you are not sure if counselling can help, call the Irish Association for Counselling and Psychotherapists and they will advise you: Tel. 01 230 0061. (British Association for Counselling and Psychotherapists: Tel. + 44 870 443 52 52.)

HOW TO FIND A COUNSELLOR

Most people are referred to a counsellor by others who have found the process a good way to work around or break through a problem. There are different approaches and it's a matter of finding which suits each individual best. Like shopping, you might favour Brown Thomas and I might prefer Penneys – both sell clothes but are very different. The initial phonecall is an important way of establishing a rapport with the counsellor. You'll know if they sound like the person who can help you.

I often advise someone going to counselling to take the first appointment as a stand-alone session. This way they can see if they like it, if the particular counsellor is the ideal person to help and if it is a therapy that suits them. Most sessions are one hour to an hour and a half long and cost €55–€70. Always check that the counsellor/psychotherapist is qualified and accredited with a relevant association/society.

FAMILY TALK

Family life in Ireland is changing rapidly. The 'nuclear' family is no longer the norm and many people are experiencing new family situations. Nowadays single parent families are common, and there is a generation growing up with 'two' families where the parents have parted but now have new partners who integrate into the children's lives.

Family counselling is similar to one-to-one counselling where a trained professional listens in a caring, non-judgemental way to the problem at hand but with the whole family present. Everyone, especially the little ones, are included. Each person gets their say as to what they think is the problem and how they think it could be best resolved. This is a fascinating way to work and often parents are amazed at the perception of their children.

Most people choose to attend a counsellor/psychotherapist privately, without telling anyone. Some people tell their partner or a close family member or friend. It is up to you to decide if you ever want to disclose what is discussed in a session. Remember the counsellor/psychotherapist will not discuss any part of your story unless in the unlikely event that someone's life is in danger. The important thing to note is that even thinking about going to a counselling/psychotherapy session is a huge step in the right direction to getting your life back on track. Many people state that having made the appointment, problems eased naturally.

MEDITATION

Often, people think that meditation is some type of strange Eastern practice that is not for them. Let's look at what meditation is and then bring it into an Irish context. The idea is to focus the mind on something simple and let all other thoughts racing around the mind relax and ease away. In the East, people sit and chant mantras (soothing spiritual words) as that is part of their culture. However, there are many other simple meditative exercises that only take five minutes and can help you to help yourself relax during a busy day.

The principal of meditation is to use techniques to bring your mind from busy and stressed, to calm and relaxed. Are there any hobbies or interests that you do that leave you feeling tranquil and chilled out? Think of something that you love to do by yourself where you lose all track of time. I bet you are not worrying when you do it. So, instead of thinking you have to get up at six in the morning and chant, you can play golf, swim or garden. The trick is to enjoy your hobby on a regular basis. If it happens to be a sport, that's great, as then you are exercising and getting fresh air at the same time as meditating.

Simple Exercise

Lie or sit down, close your eyes and think about one of the following:

1. **Someone you love. Imagine them smiling, happy and in great form.**
2. **Your breathing. The flow and ebb: does your chest rise gently with each breath?**
3. **Your favourite place to be: on the beach or in a forest. How about a scene from your favourite holiday?**
4. **Visualise yourself well, happy and pain-free.**

Many people find using a relaxation tape/CD or their favourite music helps.

THE HOLISTIC SECRETS OF ETERNAL YOUTH

We would all like to stay as youthful as we can for as long as we can. Let's try a body, mind and spirit approach and take a few simple, tried and tested tips.

BODY

1. YOUR BODY IS YOUR HOUSE just like a snail with its shell. You alone have the responsibility to look after it. Not even the richest person in the world can pay someone to eat, sleep or exercise for them. The more we look after our bodies, the easier it is to maintain good health and reap the benefits of looking our best.

2. THREE HOURS EXERCISE a week is sustainable throughout your life, even with children and a career. Remember that your body will get used to the amount of exercise you do. Exercise is for life, not a particular age. However, you may change from rollerblading to golf as you move from your thirties to your forties. You do need to do something you like or at least don't mind doing.

3. EAT HEALTHILY FIVE DAYS a week and treat yourself at the weekend. Keep treats to two meals, not the whole weekend.

4. KEEP THE MUSIC, CHANGE YOUR MAKE-UP. There has probably been a time in your life when you felt really carefree – usually in your twenties – and the music from this time can bring back a flood of memories. Play your favourite music regularly to help you to de-stress. Immediately your body will remember and start to loosen up. Your make-up or hairstyle can date you hugely. Just changing the colour of a lipstick can revitalise your look. Skincare is important, so stay natural by using products with essential oils. Experiment and have fun. Guys, remember combed-over hair will date you. The barber will help with good up-to-the-minute suggestions.

5. KNOW YOUR OWN STYLE. Play up your good points with your clothes. If you have a terrific waist but big thighs, wear gorgeous long skirts and high fitting jackets. You don't have to be a slave to fashion or spend a fortune, just pick one thing each season that suits you and accessorise wisely.

Mind

1. FULFIL YOUR WISH LIST NOW. We all have things we would like to do in life and seem to put them on the long finger. Write out the list and weave a holiday or hobby around them. If you are young, think about where you want to go while you don't have commitments. If you are approaching retirement age, a visit to relations abroad is a safe and easy way to see the world.

2. LIVE EVERY DAY AS IF IT WAS YOUR LAST. Imagine how we would view today if it were our last. Each encounter would be special. Think of the things we would say to loved ones. Why wait, do it now!

3. TOUGH TIMES HAPPEN. Learn from them and move on. Often we get caught in a negative mode of thinking about life problems. This drains our energy and prevents us from living life to the full. Remember, if you haven't moved on, there is something wrong and you need to figure out how to work around it. Get help from a good friend or a qualified counsellor.

Spirit

1. FIND YOUR PASSION. What excites you, gets you up in the morning? What do you look forward to? A clue is some hobby or interest you love to do. If you can get all fired up about gardening, travel or a challenge, your days will fly by and the personal satisfaction will be immense.

2. WRITE YOUR OWN EPITAPH. This sounds a bit drastic but do it light-heartedly. What would others say about you? Does it match what you would like others to say about you? Make changes now!

3. USE YOUR BELIEFS. Whatever your faith or beliefs are, use them. If you pray, listen for the answers. They will often come in the form of serendipity or coincidences or through nature. Ask for help, it's out there.

CHANGING HABITS HOLISTICALLY

How many times in our lives have we wanted to lose weight, tone up and change habits such as smoking that we know may not be for the best? At times we feel a great urge or resolve to change our lives in some way. Sometimes these are daydreams, but sometimes they are our inner voice speaking, and attention should be paid because at these times we ARE ready to make a difference.

The holistic way can help

This simple body, mind and spirit approach can be of enormous benefit in taking time to figure out why we really want to change some aspect of our lives right now.

1. Is it a genuine desire to feel better in myself in both body and mind?
2. Am I doing it because someone else wants me to? My partner/children/ mother/friends?
3. Is it just an impulse that will go away quickly?
4. Is it a comforting 'moan' I hide behind every so often?
5. Physically, is my body telling me I have to do something before I develop health problems?

Often we approach smoking cessation or weight loss, not with health reasons as our goal, but vanity and even social acceptance as our motivation. The effort we put into this reinforces the very longings that are throwing us off balance in the first place. Unfortunately, these motives will not help you move into a healthier relationship with yourself and so it seldom works, or not for long. The holistic approach is to assume that we all want to grow, learn and move towards making healthy, positive changes in our lives.

Simple techniques

BREATHING. A few deep breaths will relax you and help you to feel stronger and able to say no to the cigarette/ice cream/chocolate, etc.

BARTER. If you REALLY need that cigarette/piece of chocolate … have a little puff/bit of it, enjoy it, but have more fruit, more water, fresh air or a smaller next meal.

BUDDY UP. It may help to team up with a friend, your partner or family member, especially when giving up cigarettes. One day when you are feeling low, they will be strong and full of resolve and the next day it may be reversed. You can help each other.
AFFIRMATIONS. Every time you feel your resolve slipping, repeat a simple positive phrase that is in the present tense and makes you feel good. For example 'I am strong and I can do this easily and naturally'. This will take your mind off the temptation and relax you down. Try it, it does work.
VISUALISATIONS. Every night imagine yourself as a non-smoker or in a fantastic new outfit, feeling confident and healthy, just as you go to sleep. This will imprint naturally on your subconscious and make it easier to keep your resolve. Keep old photos of yourself looking gorgeous on the fridge door.
TREAT YOURSELF. If you make it through the week, pamper yourself at the weekend – not with unhealthy foods, but exotic, healthy ones. How about unusual food like papaya, game meats, asparagus, or less expensive treats such as peaches and raspberries.

DE-STRESSING

Stress affects us all in varying degrees and at different times in our lives. The stress of Christmastime or going on holidays is not comparable to losing a job or ending a relationship. Depending on where you are mentally, physically and emotionally, it is often the little things that get to us while we sail through the bigger situations life throws our way relatively easily. If we sat down and analysed why, we might come up with some surprising observations. When we are in good shape, healthy and have a means to relax, we cope better.

1. KEEP IT SIMPLE AND IN THE PRESENT!

How often do we look at the big, scary picture thinking: I'll never be relaxed, able to cope? We tend to bring the past with us, clogging up our brain with old hurts and mistakes. Let them go! We also try to live for a future better time. Hey, it might never happen. Just focus on the here and now. What you CAN do at that moment.

2. BREATHE!

Do you ever notice that when stress levels rise, your breathing gets faster? When relaxed, your breathing is always slow and calm. If you breathe slowly, you will automatically relax. Try a yoga or t'ai chi class which teach specific breathing techniques.

3. BUSY, STRESSED MIND … DISTRACT YOURSELF!

Ok, so you are breathing slowly and in the present moment, but the worries and cares are still in your head. Now what? Simply distract yourself with something you love to do (ideally not indulging in calorific treats): a hobby or interest, whatever absorbs you; a movie, gardening, walking, knitting, listening to music, reading, even your favourite soap. Pure escapism.

4. HOW DO I FIND THE TIME TO START THESE NEW HABITS?

When the children do their homework or when you come in from work are great times to do your own 'de-stress homework'. Tell the people at home that you are going to take 15/20 minutes to yourself to have an aromatherapy bath, listen to a relaxation CD or have a little snooze to recharge your batteries. Also, you can never underestimate the effect on body, mind and soul of serene surroundings: light an aromatherapy candle, burn some essential oils, play classical music, dim the lights and light a fire. You will be amazed at the reaction of everyone at home.

5. WHAT ABOUT ON A PARTICULARLY BAD DAY?

This is the time to plan a big treat. Throw yourself 100% into the tough day, but look forward to going home to your safe haven. Close your eyes and imagine that soon you will be on your comfy sofa with a warm rug to snuggle up in. On the way home get a video to cry, holler or laugh away the frustrations of the day. Go for whatever holistic treatment appeals to you. Acupuncture or reflexology are terrific all-rounder treatments and are very relaxing. The therapeutic benefits of aromatherapy massage are legendary.

6. TALK IT OUT

In Ireland we tend to keep our anxieties to ourselves, bottling it all up until we are ready to explode. Talking out a problem is a great way to ease it. Don't fall into the habit of dumping on your loved ones. There is a fine line between moaning to family or friends and asking them to listen as you get a problem off your chest. Often a solution will unfold as you speak. Take those actions! Try not to let a problem take over, instead, solve it and move on. If you think it is too personal to talk about, go to a counsellor or psychotherapist. They are trained to listen and help. It is a great way to move on and get out of a rut.

7. ATTITUDE OF GRATITUDE

Meditation is simply a way to bring the mind from being busy and stressed to being quiet and calm. At night, lie in bed and think of all the things that happened in your day for which you can be grateful. You will sleep like a baby.

PHYSICALLY

Did you ever notice that when you feel fit and healthy, life doesn't really get you down in the same way as when you feel out of condition? The idea is to factor exercise into your week, which you can maintain easily and without too much hassle.

The key to a good exercise regime is that it is sustainable right through your life. If you are out playing football and training four times a week for hours, will you be able to do this when you are thirty, forty or fifty? Your body gets used to exercise and when it stops or is drastically reduced and you eat the same quantity of food, what happens? The weight piles on and your body tone is reduced. The trick is to maintain a level of exercise which, combined with good healthy eating, will sustain you throughout life. The type of exercise you will do will vary as you get older.

MENTALLY

You know when your head feels fit to burst with worries and problems whirring around inside giving you no peace? Mental stress is the worst of all. It can leave your body feeling drained and your nerves in tatters. A relatively easy way to relieve mental stress is to think of some hobby or interest that engrosses you completely. Watching a film or reading a book is great escapism, you become so caught up in the story line that the problem or worry is relieved for an hour or two. Any pursuit which leaves you feeling relaxed and refreshed will do.

Another excellent time-out routine is a very easy and gentle form of meditation. Many of us have heard of this but don't know a lot about it and so feel it is 'not for me'. Meditation is simply focusing your mind on one thing to the exclusion of all else. You might lie or sit down with your eyes closed and listen to your breathing for five minutes. Every time a thought pops into your head (which it will) let it drift away and return to the sound of your breath. Another easy form of meditation, which works very well in a Western context, is to lie or sit and think of a special person you love or a special event you enjoyed. So for the five minutes you are thinking of something very pleasant: it works like a charm. To benefit completely, you need to tell whoever you live with that you are going to take a little time out and are not to be disturbed for, say, ten minutes.

EMOTIONALLY

The best way to keep yourself emotionally sound is to realise that your emotions are there for a reason: to release tension and feelings; to indicate if something is wrong and to help you to grow. Don't be afraid to experience your emotions, both good and bad. Remember your friends and family know you, so you should be comfortable letting down your guard now and then.

Often we hold in our emotions keeping a stiff upper lip and the 'show on the road'. This will keep the family routine ticking over but at what price? Your children, friends or colleagues will understand if you say something like 'I feel a bit low today, I just need to take it easy, and I'll be fine tomorrow'. You are letting them know that you aren't feeling great, that you know a little time-out will help and that you will be ok again soon. The last is particularly important for children to know. Also, delegate a bit. Why not let others prepare the dinner for a change?

Try a simple treat such as a long soak in the bath with candles and aromatherapy oils, a massage, hairdo, cappuccino with your favourite magazine, the list is endless. Often just the knowledge that you have lined up a treat at the weekend will keep you going through a busy and stressful week.

HOLISTIC TIME MANAGEMENT

We've all heard about time management from a business perspective, and although it makes great sense, we tend to use it only, if ever, at work. Consider making your time both at work and home more effective for the task in hand. If you look at this fascinating concept from a holistic viewpoint, it is much easier to put into action. Here are the main principles to try:

1. THE MAGIC LIST AT WORK

Always make a list of what needs to be done in order of priority. Most of us do this at the start of our day, taking pleasure as the day progresses in striking items off. The important thing to do is to factor in breaktime and lunchtime – time to eat and digest your food, time to chat with colleagues. How many times has the day passed when you realise you have just had a sandwich at the desk or even no lunch at all? We need breaks to rejuvenate for later tasks.

2. THE MAGIC LIST AT HOME

Most of us are accustomed to the idea of finishing one day by making a list for the next day. This way you don't have to attempt to try and hold any information in your head about work at home. If you do have a thought occur when you are home, write it down immediately and then forget about it. It is also a good habit to make lists, freeing up your mind from having to remember the minutiae of life. The important fact is not to forget to factor in 'downtime' for yourself, even if it is only ten minutes in the garden or on the couch watching a favourite television programme.

3. IN THE MOOD

Imagine you are at home or at work and you're not in great humour. Your list might have two tasks of top priority with three of minor priority. Rather than forcing yourself to do the main task when you don't feel like it, tackle one of the short, minor ones to 'warm yourself up'. This way you are doing something you don't mind doing and, since it is short, you will finish it quickly and feel good as you strike it off your list. By then your mood will have changed and you will be able to face one of the top priority tasks.

4. BODY CLOCK

Some of us are night owls and some are morning larks. See if you can work out the time of day you are most productive. That is the time to schedule important meetings and write vital documents, etc. When you have figured out the time of day you are not as productive (usually after lunch) then do your filing or make some easy phonecalls.

5. TEAMWORK

If you are working as a team on a project or as a family, pool all the skills and talents so that the right person is doing the right job on the team. Usually if you like a particular task, you will do it best.

6. TIME SHEET

If you have never used a time sheet, it is a great way to figure out what you spend most of your time doing. Take a sheet of paper and mark out the day in time segments, then fill in the time of the tasks' start and end. You may find that phonecalls on a Monday morning are a waste of time since people aren't answering, whereas in the afternoon it is easier to catch them in. You may be surprised to see how long you spend answering e-mails so you need to factor in more time to do this instead of squeezing it into an already busy schedule.

Remember the idea should be to work fewer hours more efficiently.

DO-IT-YOURSELF DETOX

Are you eating healthier and exercising more or just thinking about it? 'If only I could motivate myself to just get started' is a familiar cry to us all. Imagine you could cleanse your system, lose a few pounds and gain more energy before you even get to the gym … read on, it's easier than you think.

Detoxing your body is the way to start. Toxins are basically anything not natural to our body systems – smoke, pollution, E additives, colourings and flavourings in food. Over years they clog up the body, soak up all natural energy, age the facial skin and drain away motivation, leaving us feeling below par. Sound familiar? The benefits of detoxing are clearer skin, more energy, a flatter abdomen and girls, it can also help eradicate the dreaded cellulite!

SIMPLE DETOX TIPS

1. Drink boiled hot water cooled with a squeeze of lemon in the morning to prepare your digestive system for the day and gently ease elimination of the previous day's food. Great for your skin.
2. For two days at a time avoid all red meat, salt and sugary foods (cakes, biscuits, sweets).
3. Drink at least two 250ml bottles of still mineral water a day. Often we get headaches and lower backache because we are dehydrated. Our bodies are made of 70% water so we need to replenish this daily.
4. Cut down to three cups of tea OR coffee a day. They contain caffeine which is a diuretic and will dehydrate your body.
5. If you are low in energy and/or your fingernails are in poor condition, take a good multivitamin (especially after the winter months) to boost your immune system by replacing low levels of essential vitamins and minerals. Your energy levels should improve after two weeks.
6. When buying fruit and vegetables, pick your favourites as you will be more inclined to eat them.
7. On Mondays, stock up with fruit for the week and bring enough for your snacks at work.
8. Do NOT buy sweets, cakes or biscuits for home. You don't need them and neither do your children or teenagers. Get any such treats at the weekend outside the home.
9. Make sure you get out into the fresh air at least once a day for a walk.

All of these simple tips can be done over a week, two weeks or a month-long period. Depending on how toxic your body is, you may experience headaches, an outbreak of spots or bad breath for 1–2 days. You may even want to sleep a lot so start at a weekend. Go with it! The initial temporary discomfort is only a sign that you really needed to do this and will pass very quickly.

EASY DETOX HABITS

Skin brushing is a good habit to get into before your bath or shower, when your skin is dry. Use a bristle brush and stroke all over your body three times but always towards the heart. This will get your lymphatic system moving, which will naturally detox your body and especially help remove cellulite.

Detox your mind too

While detoxing the body, try to clear any worries and cares still in your head. Distract yourself with something you love to do (preferably not of the chocolate variety!): a hobby or interest such as gardening, walking, knitting, listening to music or reading.

HOW TO MAINTAIN YOUR IDEAL WEIGHT HOLISTICALLY, FOREVER

We have all started a healthy eating regime at some stage only to lose our resolve after a few weeks or even days. We need to keep our motivation and self-belief strong as we learn what works and what doesn't work for us food-wise. Here are some simple weight management techniques from a holistic perspective that really make the difference:

PHYSICALLY

1. USE YOUR SENSES

Look at the food you are about to eat and savour it, smell it, then slowly taste it. By that stage you will find yourself eating slower so your body has time to tell you when it is full. Remember all the pleasure is in looking, smelling and tasting. Once the food goes past your mouth, the pleasure is gone, so eat slowly.

2. HEALTHY EATING CALENDAR

Eat healthily five days a week and have the weekend for treats. Get a calendar and mark a big circle around the date every day you eat healthily and a big X every day you have a treat. At the end of the week you should have five Os and two Xs. A visual reminder of how you are doing.

3. DON'T EAT ON THE GO

If you are eating as you work or travel, you are gulping in too much air. This will upset your digestive system and cause bloating. Sit and eat slowly. It helps to put your knife and fork down between each bite.

MENTALLY

1. LOVE YOURSELF AS YOU ARE NOW

This is a tough one. We always think 'I'll be fine when I'm x stone'. That might be months, even years away. Try to appreciate yourself as you are now. Remember your family and friends love you exactly as you are now, not a slimmer future version of you.

2. VISUALISE A THINNER YOU

We plan holidays, homes and careers with military precision, but when it comes to weight we can't even look at point A, never mind see point B. Be realistic – at 40 it is not feasible to be the same size as you were as a teenager. Women are made to have curves. Enjoy them! Our men certainly appreciate them.

3. IS IT WORTH IT?

When you look at anything you are about to eat, ask yourself: Is it worth it? If you are tempted by junk food, distract yourself for half an hour and then, if you really still want it, eat half and balance later with more fruit, vegetables or water.

SPIRITUALLY

1. BLESS YOUR FOOD

Ever wondered why every religion in the world has some form of blessing their food? The main reason is to give thanks but also to pause and relax before eating. This allows digestion to occur and gives you time to chew, not wolf it down.

2. ASK FOR HELP

Now this might seem a bit weird, but let me explain. Whatever you believe in – God, saints, angels, nature – when you are experiencing difficulty or cravings, ask for help. It's there. Just listen and wait for the answers. They will come in the form of coincidences and serendipity. Just when you are tempted to throw in the towel, out of the blue a friend will ring and distract you until the moment passes and you are back on track.

HERBAL HELP

Many have heard the old wives' tales of love potions and brews to ease childbirth or uplift spirits. You may even remember your grandmother using dock leaves from her garden to ease the pain and inflammation of a nettle sting. For many years we were seduced by the allure of the apparent magical properties of antibiotics while the old remedies went out of fashion to all but the most dedicated. Nowadays we realise that, although very helpful for many of us, taking antibiotics for nearly every minor illness has resulted in their efficacy lessening. These days there is a huge swing back to using herbal remedies to prevent illness and maintain health in conjunction with allopathic medicines. Here is a sample of the most popular herbs and their uses:

1. ECHINACEA

This is a beautiful purple flower and its essence helps to boost the body's immune system. It is the alkylamide constituent of this herb which activates the T cells and improves the antibody action of the immune system, supporting the body's natural healing process. Most commonly taken as a tincture.

2. GARLIC

The humble garlic clove is not thought of as a herb but its benefits have been known and prized for centuries in Mediterranean countries. It has natural antibiotic properties and is unusual in also having anti-fungal, anti-viral and anti-bacterial effects. It has a beneficial role in the prevention of heart disease. It can be eaten as a food or in capsule form.

3. SAW PALMETTO

This green leafy plant has anti-inflammatory properties, which can help in the treatment of prostate problems. Hormonal changes are believed to be a major factor in causing enlargement of the prostate gland by increasing dihydrotestosterone, which increases the number of cells in the gland. Saw Palmetto gently reduces inflammation causing the gland to shrink and release its stranglehold on the urinary tract. It has no side effects and can be used to strengthen the prostate gland and maintain its good health. It is taken in capsule form.

4. PEPPERMINT

A traditional blend of peppermint leaves helps to soothe the digestive system while perking up the palate. It is long regarded as a natural aid to digestion after meals, but can be enjoyed at any time of the day as a pick-me-up. For this reason it is best not used as an evening/nightime drink. A popular tea.

5. ARNICA

This exquisite little yellow flower of the mountains is an amazing natural anti-inflammatory. It is well known as a terrific way to ease the effects of bruising when its goodness is extracted into gel form. It is also an effective way of combating arthritis by reducing pain and stiffness and increasing function in the affected area.

Eating fresh herbs in your food and drinking herbal teas are wonderful ways to absorb the best of these natural remedies. Another excellent and easy way to receive their goodness is in a herbal tincture. Each herb has both water-soluble and fat-soluble parts. A tincture is the essence of these, suspended in a small amount of alcohol, which has a natural preservative effect. Bioforce is a terrific range developed by Alfred Vogel, a Swiss man who brought organic herbal remedies to the modern world. The remedies are in a small glass bottle and you shake a number of drops into a glass of water. You drink one or two glasses each day. Always follow the instructions. Most tinctures are designed to be taken for a few weeks with a break. The teas or fresh herbs can be taken regularly as they are not as concentrated.

6. PARSLEY

Perhaps you have been using this versatile herb already without realising its benefits. Parsley contains very high amounts of the B vitamins, which strengthen the nervous system, and a high quantity of Vitamin C, which keeps the immune system working well to combat colds and flus. Parsley is taken as a fresh herb on food.

7. NETTLE

It may not be the most popular of garden weeds, but it is a powerhouse of natural nutrients. Nettle tea is terrific for weight loss as it supports the metabolism and has detoxifying and diuretic properties. It also has a cleansing effect on the circulatory system, lowers blood sugar and is a natural source of iron. Great for gout and arthritis, it helps to remove uric acid from the digestive system. The tea form is the most popular and easy to take. Nettle soup is another option.

The best source of herbal teas and tinctures is your local health food shop or a good pharmacy. Many supermarkets now have a great stock of teas and fresh herbs. Many popular herbs may also appear in homeopathic remedies, working on the principle of treating like-with-like in minute doses.

TRADITIONAL CHINESE MEDICINE

This is one of the oldest forms of healing and is still widely practised today. TCM, as it is often referred to, treats the whole body rather than just the symptoms. It concentrates on strengthening the body, and correcting any imbalance in the internal organs. TCM treats both acute and chronic conditions. There are three main treatments: Chinese Herbal Remedies, Acupuncture and Acupressure. Most therapists will use a combination of the herbs with either acupuncture or acupressure. Although there are hospitals in China today just using TCM to treat a wide variety of illnesses, traditionally people go to their local therapist to maintain their general health and boost their immune systems.

CHINESE HERBAL REMEDIES

These are an integral part of TCM and there are over 400 herbs, including roots, stalks, leaves, bark, flowers and minerals, used for specific purposes. They are taken internally as teas, powders, tablets or capsules or externally as creams, lotions or compresses. They are prescribed on diagnosis based on each client's clinical condition.

ACUPUNCTURE

Acupuncture is a form of treatment involving insertion of fine, sterile needles into the body's surface at strategic points in the natural energy field. These needles stay in place for 20–40 minutes as they stimulate the flow of 'qi' or life-force in the body to promote natural healing to occur. After a treatment you will feel relaxed and even slightly sleepy. I find acupuncture particularly good for gynaecological problems, including period cramps, irregular cycles, infertility and menopause symptoms. It is not for those who don't like needles even though the insertion part is virtually painless. You will feel a slight tingle all the way down the energy channel (meridian) when the therapist gently tweaks the needle to stimulate the energy flow.

ACUPRESSURE

This is Chinese Medical Massage using thumbs, sometimes even elbows, to manipulate varying degrees of pressure on the same strategic points in the body's energy field as acupuncture. It is very effective in treating back, neck and joint pains, headaches and sports injuries. The same principle is used in shiatsu and tuina.

Supplementary advice from *safe*food

Food Supplements: Should I take them?

If your kitchen cupboards contain a virtual alphabet of vitamin and mineral supplements, you are not alone. On the island of Ireland, one in four people is taking food supplements.

Reasons for taking them vary: from helping to enhance health in general, preventing you from feeling run down, helping to improve some perceived health problem, or even helping to cure a disease.

A healthy, balanced and varied diet is a fundamental requirement for general wellbeing. Food supplements are just that – supplements. Their purpose is to supplement the diet. They are not designed to replace foods.

There is one instance where a food supplement is always advised over food to reach a nutritional requirement. Taking folic acid is essential, prior to and during, early pregnancy, to help prevent neural tube defects in the baby.

How The Law Protects You

To protect individuals using food supplements, the European Union (EU) has put new legal* measures in place. These include:

- A list of permitted nutrients has been established. This only includes vitamins and minerals that are normally found in foods, such as calcium, zinc, Vitamin C or Vitamin D.
- The setting of upper safe limits of each nutrient that can be added to food supplements. These are maximum levels of vitamins and minerals that can be added to food supplements without posing a risk to health.
- Ensuring that detailed information is displayed on the label to help you make an informed choice.

*The Food Safety Authority of Ireland and the Food Standards Agency Northern Ireland are responsible for enforcing this legislation.

Considerations when Supplementing

Most people taking food supplements do so without consulting their doctor. If you think your diet isn't up to scratch, or if you are feeling a little under the weather and are thinking about trying a supplement, here are a couple of important points to bear in mind:

- If you are taking medication, seek advice from a health professional before you start taking a supplement – either a GP or a dietitian.
- Supplements should not be used as a replacement for a healthy, balanced diet.
- Never exceed the Recommended Daily Allowance (RDA %). This is the recommended intake that will fulfil most people's needs in one day. There are potential health consequences associated with taking too much of a supplement. For example, large doses of vitamins A, D or B6 can be toxic.
- People can experience negative reactions when combining certain drugs with supplementary nutrients. One example of this is combining Vitamin E with Warfarin, which can reduce clotting and cause bleeding.
- Watch out for wild health claims. If it seems unbelievable, it's probably not true.

Herbals

Herbal products, which also include traditional Chinese medicines, are often used as alternatives to conventional medicine due to the fact that they are deemed natural. We should, however, be aware that herbals can act like medicines and cannot be considered non-toxic.

Until recently herbals have not been regulated in the same way as medical products and so it has been difficult to assess the safety of these products. New legislation means that herbal supplement manufacturers will have to apply for a licence for their product.

Licensing will be based on the manufacturer providing scientific evidence supporting their product to the local food safety authority, or proving that it has been used in the EU for over thirty years without causing harm.

Herbal products that do not have licences must be sold as food supplements and comply with that legislation.

AROMATHERAPY

Aromatherapy is the art of healing through the controlled use of essential oils. These are extracted from flowers, seeds, leaves, bark, roots and resins and are used to maintain good health and revitalise the body, mind and spirit. These natural plant oils are applied in a variety of ways and are readily absorbed into the skin. Their therapeutic properties have gentle physiological effects.

We know from archaeologists that the ancient Egyptians used plants and herbs not only for medicinal purposes, but also for embalming their dead. Asoka, Emperor of India in the Third Century BC is said to have established centres, which equate with modern day hospitals, where diet therapy, herbal and plant treatments and loving kindness were the main treatments. The basis of these methods is still used in China and around the world today as traditional Chinese medicine. The ancient Greeks used perfumed oils for both cosmetic and medicinal purposes. They realised that plants and flowers had either stimulating or sedative effects. Hippocrates, the 'father of medicine', wrote: 'there is a cure on earth for every ill.' He used over 400 drugs of plant origin in his prescriptions. It became more interesting when Avicenna, from Arabia, came along. He was considered the 'father of massage and manipulation' and figured out how to distil the essences from the plants and herbs to make what we now know as essential oils. The Knights of the Crusades brought the knowledge of perfumes and oil distillation back with them, as the perfumes of Arabia had become famous throughout Europe.

Throughout the Middle Ages, all forms of plant medicine were used. Many gentlemen carried a little 'cassolette' filled with aromatics on the top of their walking sticks. It was considered a personal antiseptic and was raised to the nose in the presence of smells or disease. However, it was the French cosmetic chemist Renee Gattefossé who, in 1937, coined the term Aromatherapy.

Marguerite Maury, an Austrian, dedicated her life to aromatherapy and its value to people's wellbeing. She taught the first aromatherapy courses in the last century. Today, qualified aromatherapists are consulted for all manner of ailments, as well as for relaxation and stress management, as people begin again to appreciate the power of natural essential oils.

HOW TO USE AROMATHERAPY

There is a wide range of wonderfully simple ways to use aromatherapy to help de-stress, relax, revitalise and rejuvenate.

1. In the bath/after a shower. Use three drops of an essential oil in your bath or use an aromatherapy bath oil or shower gel.
2. In massage oil. The essential oils are mixed in a *base* or *carrier* oil, usually grapeseed or coconut. You can buy them made up or make your own by buying the essential oils and base oils in a health shop.
3. On a pillow. One drop on either side of your pillow. Blissful sleep!
4. In an oil burner. Three drops with water in the dish of an oil burner.
5. In a room fragrance. These are becoming increasingly popular as a way of freshening air in the home naturally.
6. Aromatherapy candles are a wonderful way to evoke a soothing atmosphere as well as to scent a room.
7. In a soap. There are lots of fantastic aromatherapy soaps available now to make bathtime or even washing your hands a sensual experience.

CAUTION

Essential oils are distilled to small amounts of potent natural liquids. You only need to use very small quantities. There is always the temptation to 'lash in lots', don't! You won't need to, and will feel the therapeutic effects immediately with two to three drops. Of course keep away from eyes, mouth and out of reach of children. If pregnant, epileptic or currently receiving medical treatment, do not use aromatherapy in any form. Store oils in a cool place, away from direct sunlight.

RELAXING AND CALMING OILS

Lavender eases stress and anxiety and soothes aches and pains. It also lifts winter blues. This is the ideal oil for your pillow.

Camomile relieves depression, insomnia and muscular aches and pains.

UPLIFTING OILS

Bergamot is a good example of an oil which will give you a quick energy boost while reducing frustration and uplifting the spirits. Other oils with an uplifting effect are also in the citrus family. These include Grapefruit which is also a terrific way to beat jet lag (a few drops on your hankie, or take a deep sniff every hour from the little essential oil bottle both during the flight and two to three days afterwards).

GOOD HEALTH OILS

Certain oils will boost your immune system, warding off colds and other respiratory infections.

Eucalyptus will clear the sinuses, while refreshing Pine will deepen breathing naturally. Place a few drops on your hankie, then periodically you can breathe through it.

Tea Tree is cleansing and heals cuts and cold sores. Dab two drops on the infected area which has been dampened with a few drops of water. Avoid uninfected areas of the skin as it is strong and will dry or lightly burn normal, uninfected skin.

These good health oils are used even more sparingly than the others as they are so strong (two drops is enough).

SENSUOUS OILS

Aromatherapy oils can get you and your partner ‘in the mood’.

Exotic Ylang Ylang will scent the body blissfully and arouse the senses. It is a seductive combination with earthy Patchouli, which balances the emotions and perfumes the bedroom. Rose is a classic romantic scent and its essential oil is no exception to this rule.

All good chemists/pharmacies and health food shops stock these oils. Remember to read the instructions.

THAT HOLIDAY FEELING

We seem to spend months looking forward to our holidays and then they come and go in the blink of an eye. Within days we're back to where we started, feeling stressed with little time to ourselves. Wouldn't it be fantastic to be able to keep that blissful state we feel on holiday all year long? It might not be as difficult as you think. Here are a few simple, yet effective, holistic tips to try out.

PLAN YOUR NEXT HOLIDAY IMMEDIATELY

This may sound a bit drastic but it really works. On the way home, still in a relaxed state, dream and scheme with your family or friends of where you would like to visit next. Even if financially it has to be a plan rather than a solid booking, it will give you something to look forward to straight away. Buy guidebooks, leaf through brochures and suss out the next time you are due time off work.

BUY THE MUSIC

There is always a 'holiday song', either a top hit played in the night-clubs or perhaps the local ethnic music, that we take a fancy to when we are away. If you go out, buy the CD and then play it on a cold, rainy day, you'll be surprised at how those holiday smiles come flooding back.

COOK THE FOOD

Try and make the souvlaka or paella you adored on holiday. The smells and tastes of the place you visited will create delicious aromas in your home. Smell is an amazing sense, which we tend to under-use and it is linked irrevocably to our memories. If you are not into creative cooking, find out if there is a restaurant you can visit that serves the same type of food.

KEEP UP THE HOLIDAY HABITS

If you love reading or mooching around markets when you are away, indulge in more of these interests when you come home. After a busy day, look forward to losing yourself in a good book. There are lots of fantastic new farmers' markets in most big towns, which could be a wonderful way to evoke that holiday feeling every week. If you tried jet skiing or windsurfing for the first time while away, consider taking up the sport when home.

USE YOUR HOLIDAY IMAGES AS A WAY TO RELAX

Here is a simple way to relax yourself in a short amount of time. Find 3–5 minutes to yourself a day, even if it is sitting in the car waiting to pick up the children from school. Close your eyes and in your mind's eye bring up a really nice scene from your holidays. Imagine what you were wearing, what the weather was like; in fact go through your five senses to really feel you are there. Your body will remember that holiday feeling and you will find yourself relaxing and even smiling. Another way to do this is to keep your holiday snaps handy and enjoy flicking through them.

ROAD RELAXATION

Most of us think of travel time as dead time, frequently becoming frustrated and stressed with traffic jams and the increasing amount of time we spend in our cars. Stress is an area that affects us all, but most of us are not quite sure what to do about it, and even if we were, where would we find the time to do it? Now here's a radical thought … Instead of travelling from A to B exhausted and tense, why not use this time to relax and calm a little? Imagine the car (or bus or train) as your very own private relaxation space. Here are a few simple and highly effective ideas to try out when the car is stationary:

BREATHING at traffic lights/jams … with eyes open of course! A very easy way to calm the body and mind is to breathe VERY SLOWLY. It is the basis of yoga, t'ai chi and pilates and works effectively.

1. Sit up straight (in the car/train/bus seat).
2. Exhale deeply and slowly. Pause for a few seconds, then inhale slowly.
3. Do this five times to send a simple message to the brain via the nervous system: 'I want to be relaxed right now.'

EYE EXERCISES to relieve eyestrain and potential headaches before or after a long journey.

1. Sit up straight and keep your head still. Move your eyes ONLY up and down, then right and left and back to centre.
2. Now slowly circle your eyes to the right, pause and then repeat to the left.
3. Finally rub your hands vigorously together and cup them over each eye. This has a warming, soothing effect on tired eyes so just sit for a few moments and enjoy the gentle rest.

STRETCHES that will ease neck and shoulder tension.

1. Circle your shoulders forward five times, then backwards five times.
2. Slowly bring your chin to your chest stretching the back of the neck.
3. Hold one arm at shoulder height in front of your body and grasp at the wrist, pulling away from the body to ease out the mid back and shoulders.

PSYCH DOWN to leave either work or home life worries behind you so you can enjoy the day or evening in peace.

1. Either before or after your journey sit in the car and breathe slowly.
2. Consciously leave any problems or worries from the previous hours behind you.
3. Imagine, as you start up the car, that the further you drive away from home or work, the smaller and smaller any worries will become, leaving you calm, yet alert.

MUSIC is a great way to soothe you on your journeys especially the long trips. Try Lyric FM or a relaxing CD.

Pick whichever one of the tips above takes your fancy and try it out tomorrow. Maybe even try one a day and see which ones suit you best. Happy driving!

THE HOLISTIC APPROACH TO PREGNANCY

Many clients I have worked with really enjoyed the holistic approach to pregnancy and found it eased many common problems, yet gave them a sense of control and empowerment. My sister, Valerie, also a holistic therapist, used these tips in both her pregnancies to great avail.

YOGA

1. A healthy lifestyle in pregnancy contributes much to your long-term health and to that of your baby. With the practice of yoga, you can gain control of your breathing and become familiar, in advance, with the muscles used in birthing. This will give you confidence when the time comes.

2. Posture during pregnancy is improved through Yoga and there is a more rapid recovery of good muscle tone after the birth. You will enjoy your baby more because you will feel fit and rested.

3. As your baby grows throughout your pregnancy, yoga is used to strengthen and tone your body. It helps you stay relaxed and adaptable in the face of changing circumstances around your life. Practising yoga opens the chest for deeper breathing, lifts the breastbone to make more room for the baby, stretches the legs to exercise the pelvic muscles, holds the spine erect for free flow of energy, steadies your emotions and helps access the deep relaxation that lies within you.

4. Yoga helps to get your body quickly back into peak condition. Yoga breathing, stretching and relaxation have a calming effect on the body and mind. You can minimise stress, strain and fatigue throughout your pregnancy.

MORNING SICKNESS

1. Sip either hot or cold water first thing in the morning to alleviate the symptoms of morning sickness.

2. Drink pure mineral waters and ginger, peppermint or camomile teas.

3. Eat fresh fruit such as pears, peaches, nectarines, ripe bananas and seedless grapes, and add fresh ginger to stir-fries.

4. Since the secret of keeping your blood sugar at appropriate levels is to eat little and often, you can treat yourself to plain biscuits such as oatcakes and those made from bran and arrowroot.

5. Avoid 'diet' or sweet fizzy drinks, saccharine, rich cheeses, liver, or foods that are chemically treated, highly spiced, fatty or acidic.

6. Absolutely avoid alcohol and smoking or smoky environments.

7. Wear travel-sick bands. They can be quite effective.

URINARY PROBLEMS

1. When you urinate, lean forward to ensure that you empty the bladder completely.

2. Limit your fluid intake after 8pm if you want an uninterrupted night's sleep.

3. Do not limit your fluid intake during the day, although it is advisable to cut down on tea and coffee because these can act as diuretics (agents that encourage the discharge of urine), which can aggravate the problem.

FATIGUE

1. Start practising the art of relaxation and give yourself a little longer to accomplish everyday chores.

2. If you find it difficult to sleep at night, practise your relaxation techniques and find time to rest during the day – even a 20 minute rest will be beneficial.

3. Get fresh air every day with a brisk walk if possible, which will also do wonders for toning your pelvic floor.

4. Energy levels can drop without warning, so do not skip meals.

CONSTIPATION

1. Regular exercise will prevent this problem occurring.

2. Make sure you have breakfast – the first and best meal of the day – as it plays a key role in keeping the bowels moving.

3. Eat plenty of fibre from different sources – wholemeal cereals including porridge, very ripe bananas (under-ripe for diarrhoea) or soaked prunes, fresh plums, apples (unless you have indigestion), pears, mangoes, and pineapple.

4. Eat regular meals and include a good variety of vegetables.

5. Put your feet up when eating your breakfast – it is amazing how effective this is in stimulating the bowels to empty.

6. Drink plenty of mineral water (still) during the day. We breathe in oxygen to give us life and we breathe out carbon dioxide as a waste product. So any drink that has been carbonated means we are taking a waste product into our systems. Also the gas, if gulped down, will contribute to a gassy system. Still water is best, but if you like it fizzy, pour it out, let it stand to allow the bubbles to subside, then sip it to minimise the gassy effect.

BREATHING IN LABOUR

1. Your breath is your most natural aid.

2. It helps you focus on contractions and relax between them.

3. Breathing properly takes your mind away from pain and energises your body: your muscles need oxygen to work.

4. Deep breathing also nourishes your baby with oxygen.

5. You will have a strong instinct to breathe deeply and if you have practised during pregnancy your learned response will kick in.

6. If you breathe well while contractions are mild, you will be in the swing of things and it will be easy to be mindful of your breath as they intensify.

7. The concept of taking one contraction at a time is very powerful. It helps you to be confident, rather than worrying about what is to come.

8. Allow each contraction to take over; surrender and breathe through it. Ride the wave as it rises to its peak, and then relax as it recedes.

9. Feel, but don't fight, the pain and use the pain-free space between contractions to rest.

10. Breathe and relax, use your breath as your anchor in contractions and as your raft while you rest, and float between them.

MID-LIFE CRISIS OR MID-LIFE OPPORTUNITY?

I used to think that mid-life only happened to people who were 'past it', settled into a boring routine and focusing solely on their careers or their children. Then one day I joined the dots and was horrified to realise that if you doubled 42 you got 84, a very respectable age to shuffle off your mortal coil. I was amazed when I realised that, yes, I was middle-aged. But, I thought, I still feel young and full of life, so what's the problem?

Around this time a number of very interesting clients arrived at my clinic presenting with no specific problem, just a general ennui. Going for psychotherapy or counselling is not something you do on the spur of the moment. It takes both financial and personal commitment. It also takes bravery and soul-searching. My clients, a mix of male and female, were successful people all in employment with a comfortable home life. During our sessions together we looked holistically at all aspects of their lives. Every one of them honestly examined their relationships, work situation and family life. Of course there was some work to be done, but overall things were running relatively smoothly. Yet something was missing.

Then it began to dawn on me. All the clients ranged in age from 39–50 years of age. They viewed their lives as exciting and developmental up to this point, and now, in their eyes, were facing a long vista of nothing followed by old age and death. Sounds dramatic, read on …

Think about it, from our childhood to our fortieth birthday there are amazing milestones in life. Most of us have schooling, followed by training for a first job, a career, first love, relationships, perhaps marriage and children, twenty-first, thirtieth birthdays, holidays. There are lots of life events to look forward to in the first half of our lives. However, when you think about it, after forty or thereabouts what is left? A fiftieth birthday, retirement and a pension, illness, frailty and death. Not exactly appealing.

We are lucky in that for the first time ever the majority of us in the Western world are living longer than our ancestors. Historically, the average age of death was sixty-seven years. It was the German Chancellor Von Bismarck, before the First World War, who set the age of retirement at sixty-five. He figured that two years was enough time to get your affairs in order. The world we live in now is very different and we are living right up into our eighties and nineties.

My male clients were faced with younger hotshots at work winning the accolades and chasing the promotions. For one of them, there were no promotions left as he had gone as far as he could go within the company. My female clients were seeing their children pursuing their dreams and were feeling the effects of not having had the time to look after themselves physically. Is it any wonder that I only had three clients in this position brave enough to realise that there must be more to life than that flat, 'is-that-it?' feeling?

It dawned on me that 'mid-life' is one of those terms, like 'spinster', that is just not sexy enough for us today. Maybe we could start by collectively changing it both verbally and mentally to a 'halfway point' in our existence. We could regard it not as a negative but as a potential positive. At this stage most of us have lots of life experience and a little disposable income. We need to make new life events to look forward to. Think about these four ideas:

1. At sixty-five take a gap year, just like the leaving cert. students, to travel and visit the places you dreamed about.
2. Look at the hobby you have let go of while you juggled children, career and relationship. See it with fresh eyes and work it back into your life.
3. Could your hobby be turned into a job? This would mean you could get two careers into a lifetime, with less pressure to perform or earn enough to pay the mortgage.
4. Remember that although we might think how wonderful it will be to retire and at last do nothing, the majority of wealthy people fundraise or keep busy in some way to give purpose to their lives. So a hobby of golf may morph into fundraising for the new clubhouse, or going to yoga class could mean deciding to teach it.

A good friend was recently bemoaning the fact that she hadn't been dancing in ages and felt decidedly old. Two people in our company responded in very different and fascinating ways. One replied 'Oh, discos, yes, I really enjoyed that phase of my life' and the other told us about her salsa aerobic class at the local gym. How brilliant, I thought, to be able to know that we all have phases in our lives and that while it may be possible to be Superwoman for a few months, it is impossible to do it all the time. We need to let certain aspects of our lives go to allow new areas to open up. However there is no reason why we can't reconnect with them if we choose to later on. Of course it's difficult or virtually impossible to have a vibrant clubbing life while rearing children, but if you do love dancing why not incorporate it into your exercise regime?

RELATIONSHIP SKILLS

We have all dreamt of a Prince or Princess Charming arriving to whisk us away on their white horse. Congratulations if you have already met them, but perhaps you could do with a few pointers on living happily ever after?

1. HOW TO FIND YOUR SOULMATE

Let's start with a question. How can your soulmate possibly find you if you haven't unearthed your soul? We all have such busy work lives that sometimes we forget to be … well, us! We forget to know, never mind, love ourselves. The trick is to find out what you genuinely like to do as a hobby, interest or job. You will become attractive to others when you laugh and smile naturally while you enjoy whatever you love to do.

2. SO WHAT ARE YOU LOOKING FOR?

This might sound hilarious, but we plan our careers, where we live, where we go on holidays to perfection, yet we leave the most important aspect of our lives to chance. Let me ask you straight off the top of your head what type of partner would you like? I bet you have to think about it! Could you name five attributes that you think you would like?

3. FOR YOUR EYES ONLY

Now here's the crux of the matter. Where does this type of person hang out? Many of us assume that we can meet future partners in nightclubs, bars and parties. Most of these are loud, noisy places where it is impossible to have a conversation. Go to places where you can meet a prospective partner as a friend. Get to know them rather than their cute bum! I highly recommend sports clubs and evening classes.

4. MARS AND VENUS

So perhaps you have met the partner of your dreams and all has gone well for a few months. Then do you notice that certain 'situations' crop up with alarming regularity? Men and women DO think differently. Imagine you come home upset after a really busy day. He is not telepathic, so you have to gently tell him what you need. And vice versa. If you need to talk it out and have a cry/cuddle/cup of tea/glass of wine, tell him! As a man, if you need space, ask for it. Otherwise she will keep asking you questions about what is up, perhaps assuming the 'something wrong' is her fault.

5. IF YOU LOVE ME, SET ME FREE

Ever had a possessive partner watching your every move? Ever had your family/friends impose their ideal relationship ideas on yours? Don't bring a guy shopping if he doesn't like it just because your parents shopped together. If you want to go off to the pub/golf with the lads, then take turns, and trade time off to be fair to both of you.

6. ALWAYS DO THE ROMANTIC DATE THING

If you have children, use grandparents/godparents to help out with baby-sitting or keeping older children company. Take time out for yourselves even if you are just catching up on sleep in your sexy nightie!

FENG SHUI

Many of us have heard about this Chinese practice or the Indian yogic version called Vastu, but what exactly is it and how does it work? Both are simple and make lots of sense. The basic principles are to keep your living place light, airy and spacious so that your body and mind and spirit are also uncluttered and uplifted. Let's apply it to one room in the house: the bedroom. Whether you currently have a partner or not, it is a great idea to create a space to nurture yourself while relaxing. There are four principles:

1. NO CLUTTER! Don't tell me you don't wince slightly every time you pass that bulging chest of drawers/wardrobe with old junk and rubbish. In feng shui and vastu terms, that clutter is also in your head and if you remove it physically from your bedroom, it will free up your thoughts to turn to romancing yourself or your partner.

2. SAY IT WITH COLOUR. Always have a favourite colour scheme in your bedroom, making sure that your partner likes it too. A restful, calming one is best, adding a splash of deeper colour in the soft furnishings. For example warm lavender walls with blue or purple cushions on a cream bedspread.

3. ALL PLAY AND NO WORK. Remove ANYTHING you associate with work. This includes files, computers, even, dare I say it, newspapers, which usually have bad news. I'd allow the Sunday supplements, which are usually more uplifting and suit a lie-in.

4. LIGHT AND AIRY. It is good practice to open a window and air the room every morning for a few minutes when you are dressed, even in winter. This lets fresh air circulate and releases stale night-time air. Wind chimes are a nice feature and are also a lovely way to hear the fresh air enter your room.

DAILY HEALTH CHECKLIST

Let's face it, we spend inordinate amounts of time thinking about what we should and shouldn't do health wise. Just imagine harnessing all that valuable time to spend on ourselves with heaps of fabulous energy to go with it? We would be different people. Often we look at the big scary picture wanting to lose a stone in weight, run a marathon, change our wardrobe. No wonder we don't do anything about it. Too much work! How about we take one step at a time with a simple daily health checklist that is manageable. We could even have a routine for a normal day and a reduced version of it for a busy day.

EXERCISE

Let's keep this very simple with a routine that we don't waiver from.

1. Do one stretch when you get out of bed. Pick a manageable one you have learned at a reputable class/gym or from a physiotherapist.

2. Walk up stairs instead of taking the lift.

3. Walk to the local shops instead of driving.

4. Take a walk at lunchtime around the block.

5. Here's the biggie: exercise for at least an hour three times a week. You can vary the type from a class to cycling to swimming, etc. That's it. Problem solved for life. On a busy day do 1, 2 and 3.

SIMPLE RELAXATION

Here is a simple relaxation technique, which you can do anytime, anyplace. A very easy way to calm the body and mind is to breathe very slowly. It is the basis of yoga, t'ai chi and pilates and works very effectively.

1. **Sit up straight (in the chair or car/bus seat)**
2. **Exhale deeply and slowly through the mouth (cooling) or nose (warming). Try both and see which you prefer.**
3. **Pause for a few seconds, then inhale slowly through your nose. Always breathe in through the nose to allow the little hairs to filter any impurities in the air.**
4. **Do this twenty times to send a simple message to the brain via the nervous system – 'I want to be relaxed right now.'**

RELAXATION

Relaxation is a necessity, not a luxury. We need a balance in our lives to calm those nerves and soothe the system.

1. Do ten deep breaths in bed before getting up in the morning to prepare you for the day in a relaxed and calm manner.
2. Focus on what you do when you do it. It's called 'Being in the Now' and means that your mind is not distracted by what comes next or what went on before.
3. Take two or three minutes time-out to daydream when waiting to collect the kids from school, in traffic jams or a supermarket queue. Fantasise!
4. Play some soothing music during the day.
5. Each evening treat yourself to some time to yourself – a favourite soap, a long bath, a good book.

Doesn't that all sound easy enough? On a busy day do number 1 all the time!

SIMPLE VISUALISATION

This is a really nice and easy way to get yourself off to a good quality sleep, which will leave you refreshed for the day ahead. Pick your favourite place to relax (on holiday, in the garden) or imagine a special exotic place (a desert island). Go through your five senses and really imagine you are there. What do you see, hear, feel, taste and smell? Lose yourself for 5 minutes in a total fantasy while you escape from reality and doze off into a great night's slumber.

HOLISTIC HEALTHY EATING

1. Drink at least the equivalent of two small bottles of still water per day.
2. Have only three cups of tea and coffee a day as they are diuretics and deplete water from your system. This means that too much of either can dehydrate the system, causing tiredness and even headaches
3. Try a good brand multivitamin for one month and see how your energy improves. The state of your fingernails will tell if you need them and if they are working.
4. Eat one piece of fruit before a meal to aid digestion and weight loss.
5. Eat slowly. Most indigestion is caused by eating quickly when stressed.

On a busy day do 1 and 3. Although 5 will help calm you down as well.

Remember to be realistic. We have all at some point radically changed our eating and exercise habits for a week or a fortnight only to give up as it is too hard to maintain. It is better to put a few simple healthy habits into effect but to keep them forever. It's not necessarily how much you do, but the length of time you can maintain it. Good luck and enjoy. You'll reap the benefits within a week, and in a month you will be glowing with health and vitality.

HOLISTIC THERAPIES

Reiki

Reiki is based on the principles of 'qi' also referred to as 'ki', aura, life-force or the body's natural energy field. When the flow of 'qi' is restricted, the body is more vulnerable to stress, and our emotions, thoughts and spirituality are affected negatively. The word 'reiki' means 'universal life energy' in Japanese. The therapy originally came from Japan and via Hawaii to America and Europe. In simple terms it is a 'massage' of your natural energy field. This extends an inch away from your body. It is your personal body space and you become very aware of it if someone has ever stood too close to you when talking and you feel like backing away!

The therapist's hands scan the client's body to locate areas of reduced vitality. Then they 'channel' the universal life energy in their own hands to ease away any tension, remove blockages and revitalise your system. It is deeply relaxing and works physically, mentally and emotionally to ease stress and the rigours of a busy life. The client lies down, fully dressed, wrapped in warm rugs, and the therapist uses a series of different hand positions above the body. Reiki is a subtle therapy and most people need at least two sessions to feel a difference. Once physical and emotional disturbances are removed from the life energy field, then body's natural healing abilities are enhanced.

Reiki has quickly become a popular form of therapy in Ireland. I think it is because historically we were used to hands-on healing from a variety of sources. It certainly rejuvenates you after a busy day and is great because it works with all age groups, both male and female.

A reiki session takes one hour and costs approx €50–€60. Most reiki practitioners would also practise other therapies and advertise in local health food shops or the Golden Pages.

Energy Therapy

There are many forms and names in this broad field. Energy Therapy encompasses all treatments that clear, balance and revitalise the client's energy system. Once this energy system (also known as *energy field* or *aura*) is functioning optimally, our immune systems are strengthened, leading to greater self-healing where required.

Reiki is an example of this kind of therapy, as is Integrated Energy Therapy, which uses the help and inspiration of Guardian Angels. I practise an ancient form called Shamanic Healing which is categorised as an energy therapy. It is hugely effective in helping clients break through a wide variety of physical, mental and emotional problems.

The underlying principle is that all our ills are traceable within our energy field. They leave an 'imprint' there, usually originating from a negative life experience. Most imprints can be cleared naturally by taking time out: meditating; being in nature, such as swimming in the sea. However, if the person is under stress or has repetitive negative life experiences, a build up can occur which, if left untended or unhealed, can develop into a chronic emotional, mental or physical problem. The shamanic healer (or therapist), together with the client, clears these imprints which are the energetic roots of the client's problem. Because our energy system is the core foundation level of our existence, underlying the physical, mental and emotional, intervening on the energetic means a condition is cleared at the deepest level possible.

Shamanic healing perceives illness holistically and tracks the source (imprint) of symptoms in the client's energy field. Once the source has been identified, a variety of treatments may be employed to clear the energy field. These may be reiki-like techniques which use either stones or crystals or 'spiritual journeying' by the shamanic healer with the client. This intuitive, instructive visualisation, in a trance-like state of non-ordinary reality, brings a path of new choices for the client to bring their life into greater health. Shamanic healing has been used for thousands of years by indigenous peoples from Siberia to South America, Europe to Asia, Africa to Australia. Many ancient cultures, including the Irish druids and the Indian yogis, recognised our fundamental connection to the natural world, and understood the interconnectedness of the energetic with the physical, mental and emotional in each of us. Most treatments take one hour to one and a half hours and cost in the region of €55–€65. Generally only 2/3 sessions are needed. Local health food shops, the Golden Pages and the Internet are good sources of qualified therapists.

Ayurveda

The word itself translates as 'knowledge of life' and dates back 5,000 years to the ancient Indian Sanskrit texts, the Vedas. It is a system of healing that examines your physical constitution, emotional nature and spiritual outlook. According to its philosophy, the body's natural energy manifests in three different ways or 'doshas' known as vata, pitta or kapha. This classic Indian holistic medicine works on the premise that we are all made up of a unique combination of these three. Though everyone has some of each, we tend to have an abundance of one or two doshas. This is determined at the moment of conception and is our own personal blueprint or pratiki (nature). As we move through life, the proportion of each of the three doshas constantly fluctuates according to our environment, the seasons, our diet, age and many other factors. As they move in and out of balance, the doshas can affect our health, energy levels and general mood.

Vata people in balance are creative and lively, but flighty, worried and fearful when out of balance. Pitta people in balance are motivated and purposeful, but irritable and judgemental out of balance. Kapha people in balance are stable, thoughtful and compassionate, but lethargic, stubborn and prone to overeating when out of balance. We can be combinations of two or three.

Ayurveda practitioners use a variety of different therapies to bring our doshas into balance. These include dietary advice using natural herbal remedies, massage using aromatherapy oils and yoga practices. In India, I experienced the delights of an ayurvedic treatment called Shirodara which involved hot oil dripping sensuously on my forehead. Absolutely divine!

Costs approx €55–€60 per treatment. A detailed consultation is done first to determine your doshas, so that the therapist can then decide on the most appropriate treatment for you.

Homeopathy

The principle behind homeopathy was described by Hippocrates, the 'father of medicine', 2,500 years ago. The word itself is Greek and means 'similar suffering'. This refers to the central philosophy that a substance that can produce symptoms in a healthy person can cure those symptoms in a person who is ill. A tiny dose of a carefully selected substance is given to stimulate the body's natural healing ability, enabling people to gently return to health.

Homeopathy, as we known it today, has been used for more than 200 years and was developed as a system of medicine by a German physician, Samuel Hahnemann. Homeopaths recognise that symptoms are the body's way of communicating to us that all is not well, and are an attempt to restore balance. A detailed consultation is taken, which is almost like a mini counselling session, since it goes into mental and emotional states, as well as the physical. The homeopath then selects the remedies, which may be taken in small sugar pills, tablet or powder form. As these are very potent and quite sensitive, you will be advised to take the remedy away from meals and to avoid coffee and peppermint tea while you take them. The effect is quite subtle and you may experience vivid dreams the first night you take the remedy. I have used homeopathy for altitude and travel sickness and jet lag to great effect. It is also highly effective for children.

Kinesiology

Kinesiology was developed in the last century by a US chiropractor who was impressed with the information muscle testing gave him. It is a non-intrusive therapy where the practitioner can monitor the energy and functions of the body by testing muscle responses, mainly using the arms and legs. The imbalances, once found, can then be assessed to determine whether the fault is structural, chemical, mental, emotional or energetic. The body's energy meridian system is affected by emotions, and any stress being held will upset the flow of energy, which will eventually manifest physically.

In Kinesiology, vitamins or minerals can support certain areas and functions of the body and these are used to enable the client to achieve a quicker recovery. Other assessments may include food testing to establish any intolerances. After the initial consultation, the therapist will place your fully clothed limbs into specific positions and then apply gentle pressure. This 'muscle testing' gives the therapist information and feedback from your body about its condition. A treatment plan may include nutritional supplements, various emotional stress-release techniques, Bach flower remedies, acupressure, gentle structural alignment and suggested lifestyle changes.

Each session takes one to one and a half hours and costs €50–€60. Kinesiology is an excellent therapy in relation to food intolerances, neck and shoulder pain, dyslexia, attention problems and stress.

Craniosacral Therapy

Craniosacral Therapy is a specialised form of Osteopathy. The body's craniosacral system consists of the skull, spinal cord and lower spine and is supported by membranes filled with cerebrospinal fluid. It is based on the premise that when you feel physical or emotional trauma, the flow of the cerebrospinal fluid goes out of rhythm. Practitioners apply gentle pressure on the soft tissue around the scalp, head and down the base of the spine removing any blockages in the fluid's circulation. It is a gentle but powerful therapy and changes are subtle. It is beneficial in the treatment of arthritis, migraines, sinusitis, back pain and stress-related illnesses. I had a lot of dental treatment as a child and teenager and had a sense that there was something not 'quite right' with my jaw, this therapy cleared it up in a few sessions. However, craniosacral therapy comes into its own treating mothers and babies after childbirth. In Sweden all babies' heads and mothers' pelvic areas are treated to ensure all has returned to normal.

index